Zephaniah: Prophet of the Covenant

First Printing: 2021

ISBN #: 9-781667-180540

Zephaniah

Prophet

of the

Covenant

The Lord your God is in your midst,
A victorious warrior.
He will delight over you with joy,
He will quiet you with His love,
He will rejoice over you with singing.

The floods of God's mercy ever rise above the mountains of our sins.
C.H. Spurgeon

Cover Art by Connell Patrick Byrne: The Day of the Lord: Wasteland

Zephaniah

Contents

Zephaniah

1

Backstory

As the Bible begins, in Genesis, we are told that after God created a beautiful, bountiful, and perfect world, He created a man, Adam, and a woman, Eve, in His image. God placed this first family, man and woman, husband and wife, in a garden that He had prepared for them. The couple were commissioned as God's vice regents on the earth. They are shown living in a close relationship with their Creator, walking with Him in the garden. Exploring and enjoying the creation. They were to be stewards of this new creation. Their assigned task was twofold.

First, they were to fill the earth with godly offspring; fellow image bearers. They were to have children, raise families and share the knowledge of their Creator God from generation to generation. They were to cultivate the good earth. They explore and discover the mysteries of this world and, with the exuberance of a child, share their discoveries with their Creator.

Second, Adam was to guard the creation. Although Adam did not know it, there had been a rebellion in heaven and an angel named Lucifer, portrayed as a snake in Genesis, and his confederates, had come to the new earth intent on disrupting God's plan by having Adam and Eve join in his rebellion against God. And that is just what happened. Adam and Eve were tempted by Lucifer. They convinced themselves that they would be much better off listening to Lucifer and joining the rebellion then obeying their Creator.

Immediately after following Lucifer's advice they realized their mistake. Lucifer's promise of life and advanced knowledge turned out to be a lie. Instead they were rewarded with death and alienation. Seeing what had happened God visited Adam and Eve and rather than disowning them because of their rebellion God did something remarkable. God countered Lucifer's false promise to Adam and Eve.

God made a true Promise. God Promised that one day a Son born to a woman would reverse the damage that Adam and Eve had brought on the world by their sin and rebellion. God said that this future Son and Lucifer would enter into mortal combat. Lucifer, the snake, would fatally strike the Son, however, the Son would end Lucifer's power over mankind by defeating death once and for all time, crushing the snake's head.

To perpetually remind men of the Promise to Adam and Eve, to remind them of the coming of a Son who would defeat death and alienation from God by His sacrifice, God instituted a sacrificial system. Throughout history, prior to the coming of the Promised Son, men were to sacrifice an unblemished lamb. This taught men two things. First, it taught them that their actions always carried with them consequences. Their sins and rebellion against God deserved death. And second, it reminded them of the Promise that one day, God would, send a Son to Eve to defeat death.

The story of the fulfillment of that Promise, as it was revealed in the history of the world, is the story unfolded in the Bible.

Keeping this backstory in mind, we are ready to understand Zephaniah's message.

2

Genealogy

Zephaniah 1:1 The word of the Lord which came to Zephaniah son of Cushi, son of Gedaliah, son of Amariah, son of Hezekiah, in the days of Josiah son of Amon, king of Judah:

Hezekiah was the King of Judah from 715 to 686 B.C. He was a reformer who rejected the lies of Lucifer. He rejected the worship of idols and oversaw the repair, reopening, and purification of the Temple; the place where God met with his people. Hezekiah **"did what is right in the sight of the Lord." 2 Kings 18:3, 2 Chronicles 29:2**

His son, Manasseh, did not follow in his father's faithful footsteps.

He did evil in the eyes of the Lord, following the detestable practices of the nations the Lord had driven out before the Israelites. 3 He rebuilt the high places his father Hezekiah had destroyed; he also erected altars to Baal and made an Asherah pole, as Ahab king of Israel had done. He bowed down to all the starry hosts and worshiped them. 4 He built altars in the temple of the Lord, of which the Lord had said, "In Jerusalem I will put my Name." 5 In the two courts of the temple of the Lord, he built altars to all the starry hosts. 6 He sacrificed his own son in the fire, practiced divination, sought omens, and consulted mediums and spiritists. He did much evil in the eyes of the Lord, arousing his anger. 2 Kings 21:2-6

Manasseh's son, Amon learned well from his father.

Amon did evil in the eyes of the Lord, as his father Manasseh had done. 21 He followed completely the ways of his father, worshiping the idols his father had worshiped, and bowing down to them. 22 He forsook the Lord, the God of his ancestors, and did not walk in obedience to him. 2 Kings 21:20-22

The next king was eight year old Josiah.

At the time of his a coronation things were looking pretty bleak for the nation of Judah. The nation had not only been ignoring God, but they had been worshiping false gods and even sacrificing their children to false gods for the past 57 years.

How could an eight year old boy be expected to rule such a land?

God provided an answer. Read the first sentence of Zephaniah again:

Zephaniah 1:1 The word of the Lord which came to Zephaniah son of Cushi, son of Gedaliah, son of Amariah, son of Hezekiah, in the days of Josiah son of Amon, king of Judah:

Josiah's great grandfather, as we have already noted, was the good King Hezekiah. According to the genealogy in this opening verse, Zephaniah's great-great grandfather was also Hezekiah. God's Word came to Zephaniah, Josiah's cousin, a Prince in the Royal Court.

3

The Covenant

And what Word did God reveal to the Prophet that He had placed in the Court of the young King?

Zephaniah 1:2 "I will completely remove all *things*
From the face of the earth," declares the Lord.
3 "I will remove man and beast;
I will remove the birds of the sky
And the fish of the sea,
And the stumbling blocks along with the wicked;
And I will cut off man from the face of the earth," declares the Lord.
4 "So I will stretch out My hand against Judah
And against all the inhabitants of Jerusalem.
And I will exterminate the remnant of Baal from this place,
***And* the names of the idolatrous priests along with the priests.**
5 "And those who bow down on the housetops to the host of heaven,
And those who bow down *and* swear to the Lord and *yet* swear by Baal,
6 And those who have turned back from following the Lord,
And those who have not sought the Lord or inquired of Him."

After God had made the Promise to Adam and Eve that He would raise up a Son to defeat Lucifer and bring Salvation to mankind, God sealed that Promise with a Covenant.

Although it is not something that we think about today and it is not something that is frequently taught anymore, all of history is Covenantal. It is the story of the unfolding of the Promise in God's world. It is through the Covenants, legally binding contracts, that God has revealed himself to mankind. It is through the Covenant that God has established for Himself a chosen people; People who were to walk in obedience to His commands and be a light to all the peoples of the earth. **Exodus 19:5**

God did not choose Israel over the other nations of the world or against the other nations of the world as a means of excluding the other nations. On the contrary, God chose one nation, Israel, to be His priests: priests that were tasked with proclaiming the word of God to all the nations of the world.

You shall be unto me a Kingdom of priests and a holy nation. Exodus 19:6

God chose to work through one nation, showing them His salvation, so that they could be a light to all of the nations.

In order to understand the messages that God revealed to all of His prophets, including Zephaniah, we first need to understand the structure of the Covenant.

The Covenant has five points.

1. The Preamble identifies God as the Lord over all of the earth.
2. The Historical Prologue recounts the history of God's rule over the world.
3. The Ethical Stipulations lists the laws that God has given to guide His people.
4. The Sanctions outlines blessings for obedience and curses for Covenant breaking.
5. Succession Arrangements insures future generations are brought into the Covenant.

We see this Covenant pattern throughout the Bible starting with Adam. God appeared to Noah, **Genesis 9,** Abraham, **Genesis 15,** Moses, **Exodus 19-23,** David, **2 Samuel 23,** and Jeremiah, **Jeremiah 31:31-34** and in each occasion, following the Covenant structure, God:

1. identified Himself as Sovereign and
2. recounted the mighty deeds that He had done throughout history on behalf of His people.
3. He gave laws by which mankind could live productive and joyful lives and

4. His people took an oath agreeing to both blessings for obedience and curses for disobedience.
5. Finally, God promised to be with and save the future generations of His faithful Covenant children.

But, unfortunately, God's Covenant children have never been faithful. **For all have sinned and fallen short of the glory of God. Romans 3:23 There is none that are righteous, no not one. Psalm 14:3** And like our first parents, Adam and Eve, **We have all gone astray and turned, everyone to his own way. Isaiah 53:6**

Nonetheless, even when God's Covenant children are disobedient, God is patient:

The LORD is slow to anger and abounding in steadfast love, forgiving iniquity and transgression, but he will by no means clear the guilty. Numbers 14:18

But His patience will not last forever. Being slow to anger does not mean that God will never get angry. It does not mean that God's patience will last forever. When God's patience runs out, when He has allowed men to pursue evil to the end of their rope, God sends His prophets to remind and warn the people of the Covenantal blessings for obedience and the curses for disobedience, **Deuteronomy 28-29.**

This is a long section, but because this key to understanding the Bible is unknown to most Christians, we will spend the time to read it.

Blessings and Curses

These are the words of the Covenant, which the Lord commanded Moses to make with the children of Israel in the land of Moab, beside the Covenant which he made with them in Horeb...

Covenant Blessing

And it shall come to pass, if thou shalt hearken diligently unto the voice of the Lord thy God, to observe and to do all his commandments which I command thee this day, that the Lord thy God will set thee on high above all nations of the earth:

2 And all these blessings shall come on thee, and overtake thee, if thou shalt hearken unto the voice of the Lord thy God.
3 Blessed shalt thou be in the city, and blessed shalt thou be in the field.
4 Blessed shall be the fruit of thy body, and the fruit of thy ground, and the fruit of thy cattle, the increase of thy kin, and the flocks of thy sheep.
5 Blessed shall be thy basket and thy store.
6 Blessed shalt thou be when thou comest in, and blessed shalt thou be when thou goest out.
7 The Lord shall cause thine enemies that rise up against thee to be smitten before thy face: they shall come out against thee one way, and flee before thee seven ways.
8 The Lord shall command the blessing upon thee in thy storehouses, and in all that thou settest thine hand unto; and he shall bless thee in the land which the Lord thy God giveth thee.
9 The Lord shall establish thee an holy people unto himself, as he hath sworn unto thee, if thou shalt keep the commandments of the Lord thy God, and walk in his ways.
10 And all people of the earth shall see that thou art called by the name of the Lord; and they shall be afraid of thee.
11 And the Lord shall make thee plenteous in goods, in the fruit of thy body, and in the fruit of thy cattle, and in the fruit of thy ground, in the land which the Lord swore unto thy fathers to give thee.
12 The Lord shall open unto thee his good treasure, the heaven to give the rain unto thy land in his season, and to bless all the work of thine hand: and thou shalt lend unto many nations, and thou shalt not borrow.
13 And the Lord shall make thee the head, and not the tail; and thou shalt be above only, and thou shalt not be beneath; if that thou hearken unto the commandments of the Lord thy God, which I command thee this day, to observe and to do them:
14 And thou shalt not go aside from any of the words which I command thee this day, to the right hand, or to the left, to go after other gods to serve them.

Covenant Curses

15 But it shall come to pass, if thou wilt not hearken unto the voice of the Lord thy God, to observe to do all his commandments and his statutes which I command thee this day; that all these curses shall come upon thee, and overtake thee:
16 Cursed shalt thou be in the city, and cursed shalt thou be in the field.
17 Cursed shall be thy basket and thy store.
18 Cursed shall be the fruit of thy body, and the fruit of thy land, the increase of thy kin, and the flocks of thy sheep.
19 Cursed shalt thou be when thou comest in, and cursed shalt thou be when thou goest out.

20 The Lord shall send upon thee cursing, vexation, and rebuke, in all that thou settest thine hand unto for to do, until thou be destroyed, and until thou perish quickly; because of the wickedness of thy doings, whereby thou hast forsaken me.
21 The Lord shall make the pestilence cleave unto thee, until he have consumed thee from off the land, whither thou goest to possess it.
22 The Lord shall smite thee with a consumption, and with a fever, and with an inflammation, and with an extreme burning, and with the sword, and with blasting, and with mildew; and they shall pursue thee until thou perish.
23 And thy heaven that is over thy head shall be brass, and the earth that is under thee shall be iron.
24 The Lord shall make the rain of thy land powder and dust: from heaven shall it come down upon thee, until thou be destroyed.
25 The Lord shall cause thee to be smitten before thine enemies: thou shalt go out one way against them, and flee seven ways before them: and shalt be removed into all the kingdoms of the earth.
26 And thy carcass shall be meat unto all fowls of the air, and unto the beasts of the earth, and no man shall fray them away.
27 The Lord will smite thee with the boils of Egypt, and with the tumors, and with the scab, and with the itch, whereof thou canst not be healed.
28 The Lord shall smite thee with madness, and blindness, and astonishment of heart:
29 And thou shalt grope at noonday, as the blind gropeth in darkness, and thou shalt not prosper in thy ways: and thou shalt be only oppressed and spoiled evermore, and no man shall save thee.
30 Thou shalt betroth a wife, and another man shall lie with her: thou shalt build an house, and thou shalt not dwell therein: thou shalt plant a vineyard, and shalt not gather the grapes thereof.
31 Thine ox shall be slain before thine eyes, and thou shalt not eat thereof: thine ass shall be violently taken away from before thy face, and shall not be restored to thee: thy sheep shall be given unto thine enemies, and thou shalt have none to rescue them.
32 Thy sons and thy daughters shall be given unto another people, and thine eyes shall look, and fail with longing for them all the day long; and there shall be no might in thine hand.
33 The fruit of thy land, and all thy labours, shall a nation which thou knowest not eat up; and thou shalt be only oppressed and crushed alway:
34 So that thou shalt be mad for the sight of thine eyes which thou shalt see.
35 The Lord shall smite thee in the knees, and in the legs, with a sore botch that cannot be healed, from the sole of thy foot unto the top of thy head.
36 The Lord shall bring thee, and thy king which thou shalt set over thee, unto a nation which neither thou nor thy fathers have known; and there shalt thou serve other gods, wood and stone.
37 And thou shalt become a thing of horror, an object of ridicule, a proverb, and a byword, among all nations whither the Lord shall lead thee.
38 Thou shalt carry much seed out into the field, and shalt gather but little in; for the locust shall consume it.

39 Thou shalt plant vineyards, and dress them, but shalt neither drink of the wine, nor gather the grapes; for the worms shall eat them.
40 Thou shalt have olive trees throughout all thy coasts, but thou shalt not anoint thyself with the oil; for thine olive shall cast his fruit.
41 Thou shalt beget sons and daughters, but thou shalt not enjoy them; for they shall go into captivity.
42 All thy trees and fruit of thy land shall the locust consume.
43 The stranger that is within thee shall get up above thee very high; and thou shalt come down very low.
44 He shall lend to thee, and thou shalt not lend to him: he shall be the head, and thou shalt be the tail.
45 Moreover all these curses shall come upon thee, and shall pursue thee, and overtake thee, till thou be destroyed; because thou hearken not unto the voice of the Lord thy God, to keep his commandments and his statutes which he commanded thee:
46 And they shall be upon thee for a sign and for a wonder, and upon thy seed for ever.
47 Because thou served not the Lord thy God with joyfulness, and with gladness of heart, for the abundance of all things;
48 Therefore shalt thou serve thine enemies which the Lord shall send against thee, in hunger, and in thirst, and in nakedness, and in want of all things: and he shall put a yoke of iron upon thy neck, until he have destroyed thee.
49 The Lord shall bring a nation against thee from far, from the end of the earth, as swift as the eagle flieth; a nation whose tongue thou shalt not understand;
50 A nation of fierce countenance, which shall not regard the person of the old, nor shew favour to the young:
51 And he shall eat the fruit of thy cattle, and the fruit of thy land, until thou be destroyed: which also shall not leave thee either corn, wine, or oil, or the increase of thy kin, or flocks of thy sheep, until he have destroyed thee.
52 And he shall besiege thee in all thy gates, until thy high and fenced walls come down, wherein thou trusted, throughout all thy land: and he shall besiege thee in all thy gates throughout all thy land, which the Lord thy God hath given thee.
53 And thou shalt eat the fruit of thine own body, the flesh of thy sons and of thy daughters, which the Lord thy God hath given thee, in the siege, and in the suffering, wherewith thine enemies shall distress thee:
54 So that the man that is tender among you, and very delicate, his eye shall be evil toward his brother, and toward the wife of his bosom, and toward the remnant of his children which he shall leave:
55 So that he will not give to any of them of the flesh of his children whom he shall eat: because he hath nothing left him in the siege, and in the suffering, wherewith thine enemies shall distress thee in all thy gates.
56 The tender and delicate woman among you, which would not adventure to set the sole of her foot upon the ground for delicateness and tenderness, her eye shall be evil toward the husband of her bosom, and toward her son, and toward her daughter,

57 And toward her young one that cometh out from between her feet, and toward her children which she shall bear: for she shall eat them for want of all things secretly in the siege and suffering, wherewith thine enemy shall distress thee in thy gates.
58 If thou wilt not observe to do all the words of this law that are written in this book, that thou mayest fear this glorious and fearful name, The Lord Thy God;
59 Then the Lord will make thy plagues wonderful, and the plagues of thy seed, even great plagues, and of long continuance, and sore sicknesses, and of long continuance.
60 Moreover he will bring upon thee all the diseases of Egypt, which thou wast afraid of; and they shall cleave unto thee.
61 Also every sickness, and every plague, which is not written in the book of this law, them will the Lord bring upon thee, until thou be destroyed.
62 And ye shall be left few in number, whereas ye were as the stars of heaven for multitude; because thou wouldest not obey the voice of the Lord thy God.
63 And it shall come to pass, that as the Lord rejoiced over you to do you good, and to multiply you; so the Lord will rejoice over you to destroy you, and to bring you to nought; and ye shall be plucked from off the land whither thou goest to possess it.
64 And the Lord shall scatter thee among all people, from the one end of the earth even unto the other; and there thou shalt serve other gods, which neither thou nor thy fathers have known, even wood and stone.
65 And among these nations shalt thou find no ease, neither shall the sole of thy foot have rest: but the Lord shall give thee there a trembling heart, and failing of eyes, and sorrow of mind:
66 And thy life shall hang in doubt before thee; and thou shalt fear day and night, and shalt have none assurance of thy life:
67 In the morning thou shalt say, Would God it were even! and at even thou shalt say, Would God it were morning! for the fear of thine heart wherewith thou shalt fear, and for the sight of thine eyes which thou shalt see.
68 And the Lord shall bring thee into Egypt again with ships, by the way whereof I spake unto thee, Thou shalt see it no more again: and there ye shall be sold unto your enemies for bondmen and bondwomen, and no man shall buy you.

4

Covenant Lawsuit

As we saw in **2 Kings,** the nation of Judah had been unfaithful for 57 years, worshipping other gods, participating in vile and shameful practices, neglecting the Temple, violating God's law: **the law of liberty, James 1:25,** designed to bring life and blessing. To remind the people of their Covenant obligations, the oath that they had taken to follow only God, God sent Zephaniah in the role of prosecuting attorney to Judah. Zephaniah's task was to remind Judah of the terms of the Covenant that they had entered into with God. To remind and warn them of the curses that would rain down on them for disobedience.

Many mistakenly think that the prophets role was only to predict the future. While the prophets have met with God and, as such, perhaps have had some future events revealed to them, their primary role is as prosecuting attorneys. Prophets have insight. They understand the times they are living in and they clearly see how the people of the nations are ignoring God's revelation. They understand, and point out for all to hear, that the ungodly are on a collision course with God's patience. **They understood the times and knew what Israel should do. 2 Chronicles 12:32**

Prophets are to be watchmen on the wall sounding the warning:

I have made you a watchman for the people of Israel; so hear the word I speak and give them warning from me...'When I bring the sword against a land, and the people of the land choose one of their men and make him their watchman, 3 and he sees the sword coming against the land and blows the trumpet to warn the people, 4 then if anyone hears the trumpet but does not heed the warning and the sword comes and takes their life, their blood will be on their own head. 5 Since they heard the sound of the trumpet but did not heed the warning, their blood will be on their own head. If they had heeded the warning, they would have saved themselves. Ezekiel 33:1-7

5

Cosmic Judgment

Look again at how Zephaniah began his ministry:

Zephaniah 1:2 "I will completely remove all *things*
From the face of the earth," declares the Lord.
3 "I will remove man and beast;
I will remove the birds of the sky
And the fish of the sea,
And the stumbling blocks along with the wicked;
And I will cut off man from the face of the earth," declares the Lord.

Zephaniah begins his prophesy with a loud and unmistakable wake-up call. Zephaniah announces a universal judgment on all of mankind. This judgment is to be total and is given in de-creation language. When we read through God's creation story in **Genesis** we see that God made fish, birds, animals, and then, finally, man. Here in judgment, God reverses the order. God announces that He will destroy man, animals, birds, and fish.

What can this mean?

Christ refers to this passage when explaining the meaning of a parable to His disciples.

First the parable:

24 Jesus told them another parable: "The kingdom of heaven is like a man who sowed good seed in his field. 25 But while everyone was sleeping, his enemy came and sowed weeds among the wheat, and went away. 26 When the wheat sprouted and formed heads, then the weeds also appeared.
27 "The owner's servants came to him and said, 'Sir, didn't you sow good seed in your field? Where then did the weeds come from?'

28 An enemy did this, he replied.
"The servants asked him, 'Do you want us to go and pull them up?'
29"' No, 'he answered, 'because while you are pulling the weeds, you may uproot the wheat with them. 30 Let both grow together until the harvest. At that time I will tell the harvesters: First collect the weeds and tie them in bundles to be burned; then gather the wheat and bring it into my barn.'" Matthew 13:24-29

Not understanding the parable the disciples asked for an explanation:

"Explain to us the parable of the weeds in the field."
37 He answered, "The one who sowed the good seed is the Son of Man. 38 The field is the world, and the good seed stands for the people of the kingdom. The weeds are the people of the evil one, 39 and the enemy who sows them is the devil. The harvest is the end of the age, and the harvesters are angels.
40 "As the weeds are pulled up and burned in the fire, so it will be at the end of the age. 41 The Son of Man will send out his angels, and they will weed out of his kingdom everything that causes <u>stumbling</u> along with the wicked. 42 They will throw them into the blazing furnace, where there will be weeping and gnashing of teeth. 43 Then the righteous will shine like the sun in the kingdom of their Father. Whoever has ears, let them hear.
Matthew 13:36-43

At the end of time everything that caused men to **<u>stumble</u>**, all of the false idols that they chased after and devoted their lives to will be destroyed: possessions, family, wealth, pleasure, self, prestige, power, homes, vacations; anything that that they built their lives around while ignoring God. Even the false religions and their gods will be destroyed: Allah, Mohammad, Krishna, Buddha, Gaia. Additionally, all of the wicked who ignored God and ignored God's law, pursuing these idols along with every kind of evil, will be judged and thrown away from God's presence.

Zephaniah's opening salvo of coming universal judgment was not only a message that his world needed to hear but it is a message that our world needs to hear and understand today as well. There is a coming cosmic judgment that will bring to a final end God's initial works of creation.

Unfortunately many of the pastors and teachers in the church today have compromised with the world and have failed to be faithful **watchmen.** In a bid for acceptance and relevance many Christian leaders are willing to compromise with the world.

The Churches modern passion for relevance will become its road to irrelevance... Its modern passion for felt needs will turn the Church into an echo chamber of fashionable needs that will drown out the one voice that addresses the real human below all felt needs. After all, if true needs are a first step toward faith and prayer, false needs are the opposite. As George MacDonald observed, "That need which is no need, is a demon sucking at the spring of your life." Os Guinness

To achieve what is nothing more than empty relevance many pastors teach false gospels **which are really no gospels at all. Galatians 1:7** Perhaps you have heard of the prosperity gospel, the liberation gospel, the social gospel, or the increasingly popular woke gospel.

There are even evangelical leaders currently rejecting and rewriting God's inerrant and infallible Word to accept the things that God has called abominations: syncretism which, serving the false god of inclusion, teaches that all religions are true; Lesbian, Gay, Bisexual, Transgender, Queer perversions of creation, which not only degrade those who practice such things but also confuse our children whom they attempt to recruit and enslave; Social Justice which purposely divides and destroys everything it touches; feminism which deconstructs God's building block of society, the family; abortion which murders children and sells their organs; socialism built on the breaking of the eight commandment; and much more.

Although he was not a Christian, Friedrich Nietzsche saw this more clearly than many Christians today:

There are more idols in the world than there are realities.

Look at what God has to say to watchmen who have abandoned their God appointed role of pointing out false idols and refuse to sound the warning for the church and for the world.

When the watchman sees the sword coming and does not blow the trumpet to warn the people and the sword comes and takes someone's life, that person's life will be taken because of their sin, but I will hold the watchman accountable for their blood. Ezekiel 33:1-7

It is serious business when God's appointed watchmen, pastors, seminary professors, and elders do not faithfully proclaim all of God's Word. It is serious business when they are willing to soft sell God's truth as they compromise with the false teachings of those in the world who are the enemies of truth.

The one tool, the one offensive weapon the Church has, is the Word of God, which is the sword of the Spirit. ***Ephesians 6:17*** *God isn't pleased to pierce hearts by His Spirit with soft words without the necessary hard words, because the message of the gospel and the kingdom of God is a hard thing to hear at first. But it is good. It is glorious. We constantly need to be shaped and molded, rebuked and restrained, reformed and refashioned into the image of God.*

Sanctification comes by God's Word, the Word of truth. But when the truth is smoothed out, it becomes something less than the full truth, often becomes a lie, and the Church suffers and is led further into the error that their flesh already craves. Compromisers are soft where they should be sharp, yet cut deeply those who wish to stand with conviction on principle. It is a clever trick and double standard that they employ time and time again. Shut down those holding the line, and give a ready and attentive ear to those slowly drifting from God's Truth. Thomas F. Booher

6

Judah's Judgment

Next, Zephaniah continues the hard words of his prophesy by narrowing down this universal judgment specifically directing it against His unfaithful Covenant people: Judah.

Zephaniah 1:4 "So I will stretch out My hand against Judah
And against all the inhabitants of Jerusalem.
And I will exterminate the remnant of Baal from this place,
***And* the names of the idolatrous priests along with the priests.**
5 "And those who bow down on the housetops to the host of heaven,
And those who bow down *and* swear to the Lord and *yet* swear by Baal,
6 And those who have turned back from following the Lord,
And those who have not sought the Lord or inquired of Him."

Those hearing Zephaniah must been have been incredulous, thinking, "this guy has no idea what he is talking about, after all we are God's chosen, Covenant people. He won't destroy us. We are the chosen of God. We have the promises of God. We claim and stand on the promises of God.

Hadn't God promised: **The scepter will never depart from Judah, Genesis 49:10**? God had sworn to David that the **ruler's staff** would never leave his line. The lamp would continually shine in Jerusalem. **1 Kings 11:13, 36, 15:4** Surely God would not **stretch out His hand against Judah and against all the inhabitants of Jerusalem.** Would He?"

In an ironic twist, God who had rescued His people from slavery in Egypt with an **out stretched hand, Deuteronomy 4:34,** is now announcing that he will **stretch out His hand against Judah.**

Inconceivable. They were the favored, Covenant people of God.

Were they not exempt from His judgment?

No.

Zephaniah lists six groups in Judah on whom God's judgment would fall.

1. I will exterminate the remnant of Baal. In other words, all who are worshipping Baal, all who were participating in the Baal fertility rituals, all who are sacrificing their defenseless children on the altars of Baal, will be destroyed.

Of course we no longer believe that children must be sacrificed to a bloodthirsty god so that we may gain his favor and blessing, so that we may be prosperous. But how many are willing to place their children in government run schools where they are taught that girls can become boys or boys can become girls, and a host of other biologically impossible LGBTQA+ lies? Or, how many today are willing to sacrifice their defenseless unborn children for the sake of education, career, addictions, lovers, personal peace, and affluence? How many are willing to use, without even a second thought, the tissue and organs of children for medical or cosmetic reasons? We may not practice ritual prostitution but "massage parlors" can be found in every major city and pornography is ubiquitous in our world. Are we so very different from the people of Judah in the pursuit of our gods?

An idol is anything you love more than God, fear more than God, and serve more than God. Never be idle about idols in your life.
Steve Lawson

2. I will exterminate... the names of the idolatrous priests along with the priests. The priests of Israel were to be lights to the world, showing the people the way to God, leading them to repentance, interceding for the people, instructing the people in God's truth, teaching the people the Psalms, the hymns of God, and leading worship. Instead they were leading people in the destructive and murderous worship of Baal and Molech. Because the priests were unfaithful, God announced that they would have no legacy, they would be exterminated and their names forgotten.

But notice, God not only announces judgment on the idolatrous priests. He also says that the other priests, **(along with the priests),** would also have no legacy and would be forgotten. It was not enough for the faithful priests of God to stand idly by when evil is being practiced. God held them responsible for their inaction. As Christ would later say, **He who is not with me is against me, he who does not gather with me scatters. Matthew 12:30**

If they had been faithful to their calling as priests and faithful to the people that God gave them to serve they would have intervened in the false practices and expelled the false teachers. Because they did not **gather** the people together under the truth the people **scattered. I saw all Israel scattered on the hills like sheep without a shepherd. 2 Chronicles 18:16**

This is exactly what Paul warned Titus about: **For there are many rebellious people, full of meaningless talk and deception... They must be silenced, because they are disrupting whole households by teaching things they ought not to teach—and that for the sake of dishonest gain. Titus 1:10-11** False teachers must not be allowed to lead the people of God into sin. They must be silenced. They and their false teaching must be exposed and they must be excommunicated from the church.

However, very often the problem is, we love our false teachers because they affirm us as we pursue our favorite idol; ourselves. They tell us what we want to hear: 'You are loved and accepted just as you are." These teachers provide us with an excuse for the idols we continue to pursue. **2 Timothy 4:3**

Luxury gives the mind a childish cast,
While she polishes and perverts the taste;
Habits of close attention, thinking heads,
Become more rare as dissipation spreads,
Till authors hear at length, one general cry,
Tickle and entertain us, or we die.   William Cowper

3. Next, moving from the priesthood, Zephaniah addresses the people who practice idolatry: **I will exterminate... those who bow down on**

the rooftops to the host of heaven. God had specifically warned his people against worshipping things that He had created:

And when you look up to the sky and see the sun, the moon and the stars—all the heavenly host—do not be enticed into bowing down to them and worshiping things the Lord your God has apportioned to all the nations under heaven. Deuteronomy 4:19

Despite this warning the people built altars on their roofs and worshipped the creation as gods. **Jeremiah 19:13** What makes this particularly odious is that through His Covenant God had commissioned His people to be **a kingdom of priests, a holy nation. Exodus 19:6** They should have learned of the law and the wonders, ways, works, and salvation of God from the priests that God had appointed over them. Having learned of God the people were to represent God and offer salvation to everyone they encountered. Instead of representing the One true God to the pagans, they learned of, accepted, and practiced the worship of the pagan gods, including Baal. Instead of being lights in their world shining forth the truth they embraced the darkness of Baal's lies.

Before we today are too hard in judging these idol worshippers, remember Christian, **you are a chosen race, a royal priesthood, a holy nation, a people for God's own possession, so that you may proclaim the excellencies of Him who has called you out of darkness into His marvelous light. 1 Peter 2:9** God has made Christians into a **royal priesthood**. He has called us out of darkness and given us the assignment of proclaiming Christ... **Him who called you out of darkness.** Don't make the mistake of being so enamored by the world that you are willing to abandon or even compromise your faith in Christ.

Also don't make the mistake of standing idly by. Calling those in rebellion against the truth to repentance while **proclaiming** the free gift of salvation is not just the assignment that Christ gave pastors and teachers. This is the assignment that Christ has given everyone that He called out of darkness: everyone He calls a priest.

A recent Barna Survey asked Christians: "*Have you ever heard of the Great Commission?*

All authority in heaven and on earth has been given to me, therefore go and make disciples of all nations." Matthew 28:18-20

The results of the poll broke down as follows:

No. 51%
Not sure. 6%
I can't explain its meaning. 26%
Yes, I know what it means. 17%

It is the responsibility of every Christian to proclaim the Good News of Jesus Christ, yet only 17% know what the Great Commission, commanded by Christ, even means. Just like Old Covenant Israel many Christians are failing to be lights in the world.

4. Next Zephaniah warns that God will also **exterminate... those who bow down *and* swear to the Lord and *yet* swear by Molech.** These folks were trying to have their cake and eat it too. They were trying to live in two worlds. They would bring their Sabbath sacrifices to the Lord. They would worship in the temple with the priests of the Lord. They would swear allegiance to the Lord. But, just to be on the safe side, they also swore allegiance to, and perhaps sacrificed their children, to Molech. Similarly, today many who swear allegiance to the Lord, are for the sake of cultural relevance and acceptance willing to excuse and welcome, even within the church, many beliefs that God calls out as abominations, **Revelation 22:15.**

Christ spoke of this very same attitude. **No one can serve two masters. Either you will hate the one and love the other, or you will be devoted to the one and despise the other. You cannot serve both God and money. Matthew 6:24** God rejects and judges syncretism. There are not many paths to the top of the mountain. There are not many paths to God. Where does your allegiance lie? Will you wholeheartedly serve the God who stood in your place taking the punishment that you deserved? Will you serve, alone, the God who gave you life and freed you from death? Or will you give lip service to God all the while serving yourself, placing your goals and priorities ahead of Christ?

5. Next, God says that he will **exterminate... those who have turned back from following the Lord.** These are people who followed the Lord but they were distracted by other things in life and turned away from the Lord. Christ warned of this very thing in the parable of the sower:

Like seed sown among thorns, they hear the word; 19 but the worries of this life, the deceitfulness of wealth and the desires for other things come in and choke the word, making it unfruitful. Mark 4:18-19

When tempted to abandon God we should stop and examine the consequences; consequences both here in this life and also the eternal consequences in the life to come. Are we really willing to trade the joy of the truth for the **deceitfulness** of the lies of the world?

Is getting along with and imitating those who have rejected the truth really worth it?

The moment a man realizes that he is only a pilgrim in this world, that finally he has to die and face God, and that there is all eternity before him, his whole outlook on life changes. Dr. Martyn Lloyd-Jones

6. Finally, God will **exterminate... those who have not sought the Lord or inquired of Him.** As Christians we are not to just drift along. Our faith and our lives are to be lived intentionally with both conscious and directed effort. As James reminded his congregation:

Whoever knows the right thing to do and fails to do it, for him it is sin. James 4:17

Such inactions are called sins of omission: not seeking after God and pursuing obedience. Not praying. Not loving our neighbor as ourselves. Not being grateful to God for His blessings. Not rejoicing.

As we will see, the Promised one, the Son of Eve, Jesus Christ did not leave the splendor of heaven, become a man, suffer unspeakable torture and death, and suffer separation from the Father, rescuing you from a life of futility and death so that you could be a nominal Christian: so that you could ignore your Savior while occupying your time in the pursuits of the world.

Silence in the face of evil is evil itself. God will not hold us guiltless. Not to speak is to speak. Not to act is to act. Dietrich Bonhoeffer

Joshua challenged Israel to rid themselves of their worthless idols:

Throw away the gods your ancestors worshipped beyond the Euphrates River, and in Egypt, or the gods of the Amorites... But as for me and my household, we will serve the Lord.
Joshua 24: 14-15

7

The Day of the Lord

Zephaniah 1:7 Be silent before the Lord God!
For the day of the Lord is near,
For the Lord has prepared a sacrifice,
He has consecrated His guests.
8 "Then it will come about on the day of the Lord's sacrifice
That I will punish the princes, the king's sons
And all who clothe themselves with foreign garments.
9 "And I will punish on that day all who leap over the *temple* threshold,
Who fill the house of their lord with violence and deceit.
10 "On that day," declares the Lord,
"There will be the sound of a cry from the Fish Gate,
A wail from the Second Quarter,
And a loud crash from the hills.
11 "Wail, O inhabitants of the pounding place,
For all the people of Canaan will be silenced;
All who weigh out silver will be cut off.
12 "It will come about at that time
That I will search Jerusalem with lamps,
And I will punish the men
Who are complacent like wine left on its dregs.
Who say in their hearts,
'The Lord will nothing, either good or bad.'
13 "Moreover, their wealth will become plunder
And their houses desolate;
Yes, they will build houses but not inhabit *them*,
And plant vineyards but not drink their wine."

What is meant by the Day of the Lord?

Zephaniah 1:7 Be silent before the Lord God!
For the Day of the Lord is near,
For the Lord has prepared a sacrifice,

He has consecrated His guests.

The Day of the Lord is an expression used through the Bible referring to God coming to judge His unfaithful, wayward Covenant people. The Day of the Lord is the day when God's patience runs out.

Zephaniah instructs the people to be silent and pay attention. He is warning Judah that God will be coming to judge their idolatry.
Your deeds will return upon your own head. Obadiah 1:15
You will reap what you have sown. Galatians 6:7-9

The Lord has prepared a sacrifice. What does that mean?

What sacrifice has God prepared?

The unfaithful Covenant breaking people of Judah are the sacrifice. Because they abandoned God they are going to be the sacrifice.

Who will offer this sacrifice to God?

The Lord has also **consecrated** the vicious warrior Babylonians as the priests. He will use the Babylonian military, **His guests**, to slay the sacrifice. (More about that later.)

When the sinner does not follow the Covenant and offer the spotless lamb as a sacrifice for his sins, as God had first demonstrated to Adam, and subsequently to Noah, Moses, Abraham, and David, the sinner stands before God, alone, bearing the weight of his own sins. The same is true in the New Covenant. We either come before God claiming the sacrifice of Christ on our behalf or we are sacrificed for our sins.

So to review, The Day of the Lord is when God comes throughout history to judge and discipline those who are unfaithful to Him. These Days of the Lord looked forward to:

First, as Zephaniah prophesied, God would come to judge Judah.

Second, the ultimate Day of the Lord for Judah, is when God came in judgment on His faithless Old Covenant people. The people who crucified the Promised Son, their Messiah, Jesus Christ.

Third, the final Day of the Lord is when God comes to judge the living and the dead at the end of time. **2 Timothy 4:1** But I am getting way ahead of the story.

Of course, the ultimate Day of the Lord came for Old Covenant Israel after they crucified their Creator and Messiah crying, **crucify Him, crucify Him, let his blood be on us and on our children. Matthew 27:22-25** After His resurrection, Christ came in judgment, honoring their request, in 70 A.D. in the destruction of Jerusalem and the temple. At that time millions who rejected their Messiah were either slaughtered or enslaved and the land was left in ruin.

As Paul explained: **For you yourselves know full well that the Day of the Lord will come just like a thief in the night. While they are saying, "Peace and safety!" then destruction will come upon them suddenly like labor pains upon a woman with child, and they will not escape. 1 Thessalonians 5:2-3**

Christ had warned His generation using the same language: **Behold, I am coming like a thief! Blessed is the one who stays awake. Revelation 16:15**

As we saw above, Christ also spoke about the final Day of the Lord at the end of time, when the weeds, those who rejected God, will be thrown into the eternal fire and the wheat, those who have trusted in Christ, will shine like the sun in the kingdom of their Father.

The Son of Man will send out his angels, and they will weed out of his kingdom everything that causes stumbling along with the wicked. 42 They will throw them into the blazing furnace, where there will be weeping and gnashing of teeth. 43 Then the righteous will shine like the sun in the kingdom of their Father. Whoever has ears, let them hear. Matthew 13:36-43

8

Princes' Judgment

Zephaniah began his prophesy speaking of a cosmic judgment. Next he narrowed the judgment down to Judah. Now he addresses the members of the Royal Court. Given that Zephaniah was, himself, a member of the Royal line, it is commendable that he was willing to obey God and speak forcefully. He was not willing to dilute or alter God's Word in order to keep his position and status or to gain favor. He unashamedly spoke the hard truth even though it could have cost him everything, respect, status, social standing, livelihood, and even his life. He was a faithful **watchman.**

Zephaniah 1:8 "Then it will come about on the Day of the Lord's sacrifice:
That I will punish the princes, the king's sons
And all who clothe themselves with foreign garments.

The princes were assigned the task of leading the nation in the ways of righteousness. Israel was supposed to be a people set apart. **Deuteronomy 7:6** However, instead, ignoring God's commands, **Numbers 15:38, Deuteronomy 22:11-12,** they had adopted foreign customs.

There is a story in **1 Kings 10** about an attempt to purge the land of the priests of Baal. A trap was set using **foreign garments... Jehu said to the keeper of the wardrobe, bring robes for all the servants of Baal. So he brought out robes for them.** All of the priests were then instructed to put on their robes. Not suspecting anything unusual the priests of Baal put on their robes. Once they were dressed in their robes they were easily identified and easily slaughtered.

Christ made reference to this wearing of foreign garments in the parable of the wedding feast. In **Matthew 22,** the king, representing God the Father, invited everyone to a feast for his Son, representing Christ. However, a guest **who was not wearing wedding clothes** tried to enter the feast. Because he was an imposter, not clothed in the righteousness of Christ, **he was thrown out into the darkness where there is weeping and gnashing of teeth.**

Are you beginning to get the idea that God is serious about His followers being faithful in all things and not being willing to compromise the truth with the hollow and ultimately bankrupt practices of unbelievers?

Zephaniah 1:9 "And I will punish on that day all who leap over the *temple* threshold,
Who fill the house of their Lord with violence and deceit.

In **1 Samuel 5:1-5** the Israelites did a stupid thing. In disobedience to God they removed the Ark of the Covenant from the Holy of Holies in the Temple and took it into battle, superstitiously believing that it would assure them victory. (Remember the movie Raiders of the Lost Ark when the fictional Germans were searching for the Ark believing that it would assure them victory in WW2?) Anyway, the Ark was captured by the Philistines. After they had captured the Ark of the Covenant they placed it in the temple of their god Dagon. However, the idol Dagon fell over before the Ark of the Lord. The priests of Dagon found the idol bowing down, laying across the temple threshold. Ever since that incident the priests of Dagon superstitiously avoided stepping on the threshold of their temples. Just like the priests of Dagon, the false priests of Judah followed the superstitious practice of **leaping over the temple threshold.**

This might sound strange to our ears but how many Christians follow superstitious practices today; horoscopes, astrology, enneagrams, consulting spiritsts, knock on wood, 666, fingers crossed, 13th floor, cross my heart hope to die, etc?

Christ condemned the religious leaders of His day for their superstitions. **They even make a big show of wearing Scripture verses on their foreheads and arms, and they wear big tassels. Matthew 23:5**

They observed senseless pagan superstitions while ignoring the Covenant that God made with them. They **fill the house of their**

Lord with violence and deceit. Jeremiah, who was prophesying at the same time as Zephaniah, accused the priests of turning the temple into **a den of robbers. Jeremiah 7:11 Violence, deceit, robbers**, does that sound familiar?

Jesus entered the temple courts and drove out all who were buying and selling there. He overturned the tables of the money changers and the benches of those selling doves. 13 It is written, he said to them, My house will be called a house of prayer, but you are making it a den of robbers. Matthew 21:11-13

God's people are slow to learn. We always require His loving, fatherly, discipline.

Why are we so easily enticed by unbelievers and their ways; ways that cannot bring life? Why are we quick to ignore the source of life?

He is no fool who gives what he cannot keep to gain what he cannot lose. Jim Elliot

9

Jerusalem's Judgment

Zephaniah began by announcing the Day of the Lord against the cosmos, then he narrowed the judgment down to the nation of Judah, next he spoke judgment against the ruling class, the princes of the land. In this section he describes how the Day of the Lord will affect the city of Jerusalem.

Zephaniah 1:10 "On that day," declares the Lord,
"There will be the sound of a cry from the Fish Gate,
A wail from the Second Quarter,
And a loud crash from the hills.
11 "Wail, O inhabitants of the pounding place,
For all the people of Canaan will be silenced;
All who weigh out silver will be cut off.

From the Fish Gate in the North wall, to the Second Quarter, to the hills within the city walls, Moriah, Zion, Opel, to where grain was pounded on mortars, to the financial district, there will be heard the sound of crying, wailing, and crashing when God comes in judgment. There will be no escaping The Day of the Lord.

Many years later, in 70 AD, in trying to escape as the Day of the Lord descends on Jerusalem, their descendants will also cry and wail:

And they cried to the mountains and rocks, fall on us and hide us from the face of Him who sits on the throne and from the wrath of the Lamb. Revelation 6:16

Zephaniah continued, even in this time of wrath and great judgment many will remain unmoved and complacent, refusing to repent of their wickedness.

Zephaniah 1:12 "It will come about at that time
That I will search Jerusalem with lamps,
And I will punish the men

Who are complacent like wine left on its dregs.
Who say in their hearts,
'The Lord will nothing, either good or bad.'

God announces that he will diligently search Jerusalem seeking those who are complacent **like wine left on its dregs.** In making wine the best wine is poured from one barrel to another to separate it from the dregs in the barrel. If it is left too long in one barrel it becomes bitter; worthless. Would you like to enjoy a nice glass of vinegar? Likewise these men have become indifferent to obedience to the Covenant. They think that God doesn't see their disobedience. They have convinced themselves that **The Lord will do nothing, either good or bad.**

In answer to this God announces that they will lose their wealth. The homes that they build and the vineyards that they planted, and even the wine that they produced, will all be taken away and given to their conquers, the Babylonians.

Zephaniah 1:13 "Moreover, their wealth will become plunder
And their houses desolate;
Yes, they will build houses but not inhabit *them*,
And plant vineyards but not drink their wine."

As Christ would ask centuries later, **what shall it profit a man, if he shall gain the whole world but lose his own soul? Mark 8:36** The complacent citizens of Judah had become secure in their wealth, believing that God would never judge their Covenant breaking. Of course, people claiming to be Christians frequently live the same way today. They say they believe in Christ but live as practical atheists, or as pagans chasing after false gods, as if God didn't see their every action and hear their every thought. In the final Day of the Lord, at the end of time, Christ tells such people to, **depart from Me because I never knew you, you workers of lawlessness. Matthew 7:21-23**

Zephaniah continues, stacking up judgments against Judah **because they have sinned against the Lord. Zephaniah 1:17**

Zephaniah 1:14 Near is the great day of the Lord,

Near and coming very quickly;
Listen, the day of the Lord!
In it the warrior cries out bitterly.
15 A day of wrath is that day,
A day of trouble and distress,
A day of destruction and desolation,
A day of darkness and gloom,
A day of clouds and thick darkness,
16 A day of trumpet and battle cry
Against the fortified cities
And the high corner towers.
17 I will bring distress on men
So that they will walk like the blind,
Because they have sinned against the Lord;
And their blood will be poured out like dust
And their flesh like dung.
18 Neither their silver nor their gold
Will be able to deliver them
On the day of the Lord's wrath;
And all the earth will be devoured
In the fire of His jealousy,
For He will make a complete end,
Indeed a terrifying one,
Of all the inhabitants of the earth.

What is awaiting those who break the Covenant?

Wrath, trouble, distress, destruction, desolation, darkness, gloom, blindness, blood poured out, flesh like dung, devoured, and terror, are the terrible and swift judgments awaiting those who continue to break the Covenant.

Are you a Covenant breaker deserving these judgments?

Have you ever sinned?

Have you ever been ashamed of Christ?

Have you ever compromised, going along with the sins of your friends, family, or coworkers to fit in?

Have you ever felt ashamed of your behavior?

If so, like Judah, you are a Covenant breaker, deserving the judgment of God.

Do you fear the Day of the Lord?

If you are paying attention you should deathly fear the sure and promised coming Day of the Lord.

Although I am jumping way ahead in the prophesy of Zephaniah, I can't help myself because there is unbelievably good news embedded in the Covenant. **When God made His [Covenant] Promise to Abraham... He swore by Himself saying I will bless you... Hebrews 6:13-15.** This means that **even when we are faithless He remains faithful. 2 Timothy 2:13**

How can this be? How can God be faithful and willing to save even His sinful children?

As we have seen, in the Old Covenant, from the time of Adam, a lamb was sacrificed for the sins of the people. Sin is not to be taken lightly. Sin against the Creator is deadly serious and requires sacrifice. Sin requires death. This looked forward to the New Covenant where we learn that the Old Covenant lamb actually was a placeholder looking forward to the Promised Son, Jesus Christ. The Son of God, born of a woman, just like the Promise to Adam and Eve had predicted, was the ultimate sacrifice on our behalf. He was the sacrifice that defeated death and crushed the original rebel, Lucifer. Because of this the multitudes in all of creation now sing:

Worthy is the Lamb who was slain. Revelation 5:11

Salvation is possible because in the New Covenant, God Himself, in the person of Christ, stood in our place absorbing **wrath, trouble, distress, destruction, desolation, darkness, gloom, blindness,**

blood poured out, flesh like dung, devoured, terror, and every other of the terrible and swift judgments that we rightly deserved.

For God made Christ who knew no sin *to be* sin for us, that we might become the righteousness of God in Him. 2 Corinthians 5:21

Everyone who has ever lived will, one day, stand before God to be judged. This will only go either one of two ways. You will stand before God in your own strength, your thoughts and deeds exposed. In which case you will bear the weight of your sin, as **Zephaniah 1:7** puts it, you will be the **sacrifice;** slaughtered.

Or you will come before God the Father represented by Christ standing in your place.

Christ who knew no sin *to be* sin for us, that we might become the righteousness of God in Him. 2 Corinthians 5:21

Christ bore the **Wrath of the Lord** in your place. Christ stood for you on **The Day of the Lord.** Christ was the **sacrifice,** the Lamb of God.

There is no place to hide but in the blood of the Lamb. A.W. Tozer

10

Call to Repentance

Zephaniah, had come before the King and his Court with a message directly from God: a message of doom.

If you were the King or one of the Kings trusted advisors what would your immediate reaction be to such a message?

What would you advise the King to do?

What should the King do?

If I were the King, I would ask Zephaniah if there was anything that could be done to forestall the coming Day of the Lord.

How can we as a nation make this right?

How can we satisfy the wrath of God?

That must have been exactly what the King and his advisors did. Listen to Zephaniah's response.

Zephaniah 2:1 Gather yourselves together like stubble,
yes, gather together like stubble,
O nation without shame,
2 Before the decree takes effect—
The day passes like the chaff—
Before the burning wrath of the Lord comes upon you,
Before the day of the Lord's anger comes upon you.
3 Seek the Lord,
All you humble in the land
You who do His justice;
Seek righteousness, seek humility.
Perhaps you will be hidden
In the day of the Lord's wrath

Zephaniah gives the leaders five commands. They are to **gather** themselves, **seek the Lord, do justice, seek righteousness,** and **seek humility.**

1. Throughout the Bible, self-confident, shameless, people are likened to stubble ready for the judgment of burning. For example, **Surely the day is coming; it will burn like a furnace. All the arrogant and every evildoer will be stubble, and the day that is coming will set them on fire. Malachi 4:1** These shameless people must **gather** themselves, acknowledge their guilt, change their behavior, and stop worshipping and sacrificing to false gods. And they must do this quickly. Their situation is urgent. They must repent and change their behavior **before God's decree takes effect.** How are they to do this?

Are today's pastors and teachers in the West urging the church to gather themselves and flee from their shameful, evil, attitudes and behavior before God comes in judgment?

2. They are told to **seek the Lord.** The only refuge from the wrath of God is to be found in God. God is our only shelter. No one can hide from God. They can't run away. They can't hide under the mountains. **They called to the mountains, fall on us, hide us from the wrath... Revelation 6:16** But that didn't work. As Christ advised the people of Israel, they were to **seek first the kingdom of God and his righteousness. Matthew 6:33** Seeking anything else, fame, wealth, security, immortality, pleasure, is ultimately futile because those things cannot protect you from the wrath of God.

And where may God be found?

God may be found in His Word: **Your Word is a lamp to my feet and a light for my path. Psalm 119:105** Immerse yourself in God's Word. It was written to speak His words of life to you.

God may be found in prayer: **The Lord is near to all who call on Him. Psalm 145:18** God wants to be with you. **The Lord takes pleasure in His people. Psalm 149:4**

3. They are told to **do justice.** Some 50 years earlier the prophet Amos had admonished Judah to, **Let justice roll on like a river... a never failing stream. Amos 5:24** Like a river is always flowing, justice should always be upheld in the land. Apparently, this was a lesson that Judah still needed to learn.

To do justice means that everyone is to be treated equally under the law. The problem is, as Bruce Cockburn cleverly observed:

Everybody wants to see justice done on somebody else.

In other words, I'm all for everyone getting justice as long as it doesn't cost me anything.

Here is what the Bible says about justice.

It is wrong to show favoritism when passing judgment, when attempting to right wrongs. Proverbs 24:23

Do not pervert justice by siding with the crowd, and do not show favoritism to the poor in a lawsuit. Exodus 23:2-3

Do not pervert justice; do not show partiality to the poor or favoritism to the great, but judge your neighbor fairly. Leviticus 19:15

The wealthy are not to be favored while the poor are exploited. This would mean, especially in the context of the ongoing child sacrifices to Molech and Baal, the weakest in the land, the children, were not to be slaughtered in an attempt to gain the blessing of those gods.

But notice also, the poor are not to be favored over the wealthy. Justice means that everyone is treated equally. That is why in the West Lady Justice is depicted wearing a blindfold. Although this is better saved for another time, because our modern idol of Social Justice seeks equity instead of equality, it is false and destructive. There is no such thing as Social Justice in the Bible.

4. They are told to **seek righteousness.**

Righteousness exalts a nation, but sin is a disgrace to any people. Proverbs 14:24

What is righteousness?

God defines righteousness in the Covenant that He made with His people:

And it shall come to pass, if thou shalt hearken diligently unto the voice of the Lord thy God, to observe and to do all his commandments which I command thee this day, that the Lord thy God will set thee on high above all nations of the earth. Deuteronomy 28:1

Zephaniah advises the King to **seek** to understand and follow all of God's commands. The problem that Josiah faced was that for generations the priests and prophets had led the people away from God's truth and into sin. As we will see shortly, God's Word had even been misplaced and lost.

5. They are to **seek humility.**

After generations of ignoring and disobeying the true God while honoring worthless idols, the people had become arrogant. They had come to believe that they controlled their own destiny. If they worshiped the right gods in the right way they could coerce blessing. They controlled the gods by their superstitious actions. The true God was not part of their equation. As we saw above, they deceived themselves saying: **The Lord will do nothing, either good or bad. Zephaniah 1:12**

Zephaniah was advising the people to: **humble yourselves before the Lord, and He will lift you up. James 4:10**

And these things, **seeking the Lord, doing justice, seeking righteousness,** and **seeking humility** are exactly what Josiah did. He took Zephaniah's admonition to heart. He initiated a widespread Reformation. **2 Kings 22-23**

The first thing that Josiah did was to order the renovation of the temple. In the process of renovation the lost Word of God was discovered.

Hilkiah the high priest said to Shaphan the secretary, "I have found the Book of the Law in the temple of the Lord." He gave it to Shaphan, who read it. Then Shaphan the secretary informed the king, "Hilkiah the priest has given me a book." And Shaphan read from it in the presence of the king.
When the king heard the words of the Book of the Law, he tore his robes. He gave these orders to Hilkiah the priest, Ahikam son of Shaphan, Akbor son of Micaiah, Shaphan the secretary and Asaiah the king's attendant: "Go and inquire of the Lord for me and for the people and for all Judah about what is written in this book that has been found. Great is the Lord's anger that burns against us because those who have gone before us have not obeyed the words of this book; they have not acted in accordance with all that is written there concerning us." 2 Kings 22:8-13

Then the king called together all the elders of Judah and Jerusalem. 2 He went up to the temple of the Lord with the people of Judah, the inhabitants of Jerusalem, the priests and the prophets—all the people from the least to the greatest. He read in their hearing all the words of the Book of the Covenant, which had been found in the temple of the Lord. 3 The king stood by the pillar and renewed the Covenant in the presence of the Lord—to follow the Lord and keep his commands, statutes and decrees with all his heart and all his soul, thus confirming the words of the Covenant written in this book. Then all the people pledged themselves to the Covenant.
4 The king ordered Hilkiah the high priest, the priests next in rank and the doorkeepers to remove from the temple of the Lord all the articles made for Baal and Asherah and all the starry hosts. He burned them outside Jerusalem in the fields of the Kidron Valley and took the ashes to Bethel. 5 He did away with

the idolatrous priests appointed by the kings of Judah to burn incense on the high places of the towns of Judah and on those around Jerusalem—those who burned incense to Baal, to the sun and moon, to the constellations and to all the starry hosts. 6 He took the Asherah pole from the temple of the Lord to the Kidron Valley outside Jerusalem and burned it there. He ground it to powder and scattered the dust over the graves of the common people. 7 He also tore down the quarters of the male shrine prostitutes that were in the temple of the Lord, the quarters where women did weaving for Asherah.

8 Josiah brought all the priests from the towns of Judah and desecrated the high places, from Geba to Beersheba, where the priests had burned incense. He broke down the gateway at the entrance of the Gate of Joshua, the city governor, which was on the left of the city gate. 9 Although the priests of the high places did not serve at the altar of the Lord in Jerusalem, they ate unleavened bread with their fellow priests.

10 He desecrated Topheth, which was in the Valley of Ben Hinnom, so no one could use it to sacrifice their son or daughter in the fire to Molek. 11 He removed from the entrance to the temple of the Lord the horses that the kings of Judah had dedicated to the sun. They were in the court near the room of an official named Nathan-Melek. Josiah then burned the chariots dedicated to the sun.

12 He pulled down the altars the kings of Judah had erected on the roof near the upper room of Ahaz, and the altars Manasseh had built in the two courts of the temple of the Lord. He removed them from there, smashed them to pieces and threw the rubble into the Kidron Valley. 13 The king also desecrated the high places that were east of Jerusalem on the south of the Hill of Corruption—the ones Solomon king of Israel had built for Ashtoreth the vile goddess of the Sidonians, for Chemosh the vile god of Moab, and for Molek the detestable god of the people of Ammon. 14 Josiah smashed the sacred stones and cut down the Asherah poles and covered the sites with human bones.

15 Even the altar at Bethel, the high place made by Jeroboam son of Nebat, who had caused Israel to sin—even that altar and high place he demolished. He burned the high place and ground it to powder, and burned the Asherah pole also. 16 Then Josiah looked

around, and when he saw the tombs that were there on the hillside, he had the bones removed from them and burned on the altar to defile it, in accordance with the word of the Lord proclaimed by the man of God who foretold these things.
17 The king asked, "What is that tombstone I see?"
The people of the city said, "It marks the tomb of the man of God who came from Judah and pronounced against the altar of Bethel the very things you have done to it."
18 "Leave it alone," he said. "Don't let anyone disturb his bones." So they spared his bones and those of the prophet who had come from Samaria.
19 Just as he had done at Bethel, Josiah removed all the shrines at the high places that the kings of Israel had built in the towns of
Samaria and that had aroused the Lord's anger. 20 Josiah
slaughtered all the priests of those high places on the altars and burned human bones on them. Then he went back to Jerusalem.
21 The king gave this order to all the people: "Celebrate the Passover to the Lord your God, as it is written in this Book of the
Covenant." 22 Neither in the days of the judges who led Israel nor in the days of the kings of Israel and the kings of Judah had any such Passover been observed. 23 But in the eighteenth year of King Josiah, this Passover was celebrated to the Lord in Jerusalem.
24 Furthermore, Josiah got rid of the mediums and spiritists, the household gods, the idols and all the other detestable things seen in Judah and Jerusalem. This he did to fulfill the requirements of the law written in the book that Hilkiah the priest had discovered in the temple of the Lord. 25 Neither before nor after Josiah was there a king like him who turned to the Lord as he did—with all his heart and with all his soul and with all his strength, in accordance with all the Law of Moses. 2 Kings 23

Because Josiah had sought after the Lord, humbled himself, pursued justice, and righteousness, God spared Josiah, and spared his kingdom from His wrath, forestalling the promised Day of the Lord. However, this reprieve was short lived.

Sadly, both of Josiah's sons who reigned after him, Jehoahaz and Eliakim, again did evil in the eyes of the Lord. It was during Eliakim's reign that the Lord brought the army of Babylon against Judah, ransacking the land and carrying the people off into slavery, just as God had warned Manasseh.

The history of the human race is the history of the relentless resistance by human beings to the sweetness to the grace of God.
R.C. Sproul

However, because Josiah obediently pursued God, God withheld judgment.

The Lord is gracious and compassionate, slow to anger, abounding in mercy. Psalm 145:8

11

Nation's Judgment

God not only judges His people, God also judges other nations. Just because the other nations were not blessed with God's special revelation, the Bible, as Judah had been, doesn't mean that they are free to do whatever they please. God never allows ignorance as an excuse for unchecked sin in a nation. Paul addressed this 'excuse', this rationalization, extensively in his letter to the Romans.

18 The wrath of God is being revealed from heaven against all the godlessness and wickedness of people, who suppress the truth by their wickedness, 19 since what may be known about God is plain to them, because God has made it plain to them. 20 For since the creation of the world God's invisible qualities—his eternal power and divine nature—have been clearly seen, being understood from what has been made, so that people are without excuse... 14 (Indeed, when Gentiles, who do not have the law, do by nature things required by the law, they are a law for themselves, even though they do not have the law. 15 They show that the requirements of the law are written on their hearts, their consciences also bearing witness, and their thoughts sometimes accusing them and at other times even defending them.) Romans 1:18-20; 2:14-15

The peoples of the nations are accountable to God even if they don't have the Bible. They **suppress the truth** that has given them. They have no **excuse**. God has given everyone a conscience. Everyone, made in God's image, is able to recognize the difference between right and wrong; good and evil. In fact it is **clearly seen** and **understood.**

When we see rampant evil in the world; tyranny, injustice, violence, mass murder, racism, slavery, sex trafficking, the widespread ignoring of God's design for marriage, family, economics, LBTQA+s shamelessly proclaiming their perversions, and much more, it is easy to get overwhelmed. It is easy to feel hopeless. It is easy to question:

What is God doing?

God is being patient. Don't mistake God's patience for His inaction or inability to act. God is always in control.

The king's heart is in the hand of the Lord. He turns it wherever He wishes. Proverbs 21:1

Judgment will come to those who refuse to repent, turn, and walk in God's way.

Just as Zephaniah had warned Josiah that, after generations of sin, rebellion, and whoring after other gods, His patience with Judah had run out, God comes in judgment against the nations. God's patience had run out and it was time for a clean sweep. Zephaniah addresses the nations surrounding Judah; the nations to the North, South, East, and West.

And just to be clear, God tells us that when He comes to shake a nation only those things that cannot be shaken will remain.

And this word, Yet once more, signifies the removing of those things that are shaken, as of things that are made, that those things which cannot be shaken may remain. Hebrews 12:27

All the false things that people place their faith in, all the hollow things that people count on for their security, will be shaken by God. After the shaking only the things that are true will remain. This should serve as a warning today, not only for our world and it's many empty pursuits and false beliefs, but it should also serve as a warning to the churches that embrace and incorporate the teaching of the world. The church will be shaken to sort out the false from the faithful. Only the faithful will remain steadfast. The faithful have nothing to fear.

God's Judgment on Philistia

Zephaniah 2:4 For Gaza will be abandoned
And Ashkelon a desolation;
Ashdod will be driven out at noon
And Ekron will be uprooted.
5 Woe to the inhabitants of the seacoast,
The nation of the Cherethites!
The word of the Lord is against you,
O Canaan, land of the Philistines;
And I will destroy you
So that there will be no inhabitant.
6 So the seacoast will be pastures,
***With* caves for shepherds and folds for flocks.**
7 And the coast will be
For the remnant of the house of Judah,
They will pasture on it.
In the houses of Ashkelon they will lie down at evening;
For the Lord their God will care for them
And restore their fortune.

God announces judgment against the four main cities of Philistia, Gaza, Ashkelon, Ashdod, and Enron, as well as those living on the sea coast. We are not told why God is uprooting the Philistines but perhaps it has some connection to when the Prophet Amos condemned them some 50 years earlier.

Because she took captive whole communities and sold them into slavery. Amos 1:6

Philistia profited from human slave trade. They would capture whole communities and sell the captives into slavery. God expects even pagan nations to recognize and uphold basic human rights. Justice matters to God. He will not indefinitely overlook nations that ignore human rights. He will not overlook those nations that practice slavery.

In an example close to home; God came in judgment against the United States, shaking the land, at the cost of almost a million lives, for engaging in the sin of slavery. **Exodus 21:16** This should also stand as a warning to all those Muslim nations that continue to practice slavery today as their false god, Allah, teaches in the Quran. This should stand as a warning to the Chinese who continue to enslave people today. And this should stand as a warning to all corporations who are currently profiting from the exploitation of Chinese slave labor.

It is interesting that in the judgment against Philistia God includes a note of hope **for the remnant of the house of Judah**. The remnant will be gifted the land of Philistia. Even after judging Judah, **the Lord their God will care for them and restore their fortunes.**

This is a picture of the love that God always showers on His Covenant children. Even when we are **faithless, God remains faithful.**
2 Timothy 2:13 Yes, as we saw, after Josiah, the people will again fall into heinous sin, but even in that, at the time of their exile into Babylon, God will preserve a remnant. **The Lord their God will care for them and restore their fortunes.**

God's Judgment on Moab

Zephaniah 2:8 "I have heard the taunting of Moab
And the revilings of the sons of Ammon,
With which they have taunted My people
And become arrogant against their territory.
9 "Therefore, as I live," declares the Lord of hosts,
The God of Israel,
"Surely Moab will be like Sodom
And the sons of Ammon like Gomorrah—
A place possessed by nettles and salt pits,
And a perpetual desolation.
The remnant of My people will plunder them
And the remainder of My nation will inherit them."
10 This they will have in return for their pride, because they have taunted and become arrogant against the people of the Lord of hosts. 11 The Lord will be terrifying to them, for He will starve all the gods of the earth; and all the coastlands of the nations will bow down to Him, everyone from his *own* place.

The people of Moab were proud in their own strength. In their pride they mocked and taunted the people of God. In reviling the people of God they were also arrogantly mocking the Lord of Hosts… never a good idea. Because of their actions God said that he would terrify them. He would terrify them by destroying their gods. The gods that they believed in and counted on for security and blessing were going to be exposed as worthless.

As Paul reminded the pagan Corinthians: **We know that "An idol is nothing at all in the world" and that "There is no God but one." 5 For even if there are so-called gods, whether in heaven or on earth (as indeed there are many "gods" and many "lords"), 6 yet for us there is but one God, the Father, from whom all things came and for whom we live; and there is but one Lord, Jesus Christ, through whom all things came and through whom we live. 1 Corinthians 8:4-6**

Idols are worthless and God was going to show Moab just that.

Are there people in the world today who mock God and taunt those who believe in Him?

What should the Christians response be to such mocking?

We can take comfort in the sure knowledge that the situation is never beyond God's control. God's truth always will prevail. We should pray that they come to their senses and stop mocking the only One who can give them life. As Christ prayed: **Father forgive them for they know not what they do. Luke 23:43**

Here again, Zephaniah concluded his judgment against Moab with a promise to the faithful remnant of Judah. **The remnant of My people will plunder them, And the remainder of My nation will inherit them."** After God judges Moab the faithful in Judah will inherit their land in fulfillment of the promise found in **Proverbs 13:22:**

A good man leaves an inheritance to his children's children:
But the wealth of the sinner is laid up for the just. Proverbs 13:22

God's Judgment on Cush

12 "You also, O Cush, will be slain by My sword."

Cush was located in what is today Southern Egypt, Ethiopia, and Sudan. Again, God does not tell us here why Cush would be slain, however, the Prophet Ezekiel, speaking some 20 years after Zephaniah, condemned Cush for her complacency. **Ezekiel 30:9** Just as Zephaniah had prophesied that God would punish Judah for complacency, Cush practiced the same sin, believing that they could get along just find in the world by ignoring the law that God had placed in their hearts. They suppressed God's truth, the truth that He had made known to them. In exchange they jettisoned what was clearly seen and understood and invented their own truth. God had given them a conscience and He intended for them to follow it.

Christ himself had brought this very same charge against His church in Laodicea. **I know your deeds, that you are neither cold nor hot. I wish you were either one or the other! So, because you are lukewarm - neither hot nor cold - I am about to spit you out of my mouth. Revelation 3:15-16**

The nations are never to be complacent. Ignoring the truth brings with it consequences from the throne of God. That is also why Christians are never to quietly blend in with the culture. Christians are to call the world to repentance, imploring them to take stock of their sins. We are to instruct, heal, and love, as we are vocal witnesses to the salvation of Christ to a lost and hurting world. Again, as Christ reminded His disciples:

You are the salt of the earth. But if the salt loses its saltiness, how can it be made salty again? It is no longer good for anything, except to be thrown out and trampled underfoot. Matthew 5:13

God's Judgment on Assyria

Zephaniah 2:13 And He will stretch out His hand against the north
And destroy Assyria,
And He will make Nineveh a desolation,
Parched like the wilderness.
14 Flocks will lie down in her midst,
All beasts which range in herds;
Both the pelican and the hedgehog
Will lodge in the tops of her pillars;
Birds will sing in the window,
Desolation *will be* on the threshold;
For He has laid bare the cedar work.
15 This is the exultant city
Which dwells securely,
Who says in her heart,
"I am, and there is no one besides me."
How she has become a desolation,
A resting place for beasts!
Everyone who passes by her will hiss
***And* wave his hand *in contempt*.**

Assyria boasted in her self-sufficiency: **I am, and there is no one besides me.** In her arrogance she thought that she was secure in following her idols. She believed that there was no need of God. Again, just as Christ had warned His church at Laodicea, saying, **You say, I am rich; I have acquired wealth and do not need a thing. But you do not realize that you are wretched, pitiful, poor, blind, and naked. Revelation 3:17**

In **Psalm 2** David explains that the people of the nations of the world and their rulers arrogantly conspire and plot to escape God's control over their lives. Assyria boasts, **I am, and there is none besides me.** Laodicea boasts, **I am rich... I do not need a thing.** Similarly, nations of the world today mock God and His standards, and conspire against God's children, persecuting, silencing, imprisoning, and murdering them.

What is God's response?

Why do the nations conspire
and the peoples plot in vain?
The kings of the earth rise up
and the rulers band together
against the Lord and against his anointed, saying,
"Let us break their chains
and throw off their shackles."
The One enthroned in heaven laughs;
the Lord scoffs at them.
He rebukes them in his anger
and terrifies them in his wrath, saying,
"I have installed my king
on Zion, my holy mountain."

God laughs at their arrogance. God scoffs at them and when His gracious patience runs out He **rebukes them in His anger and terrifies them in His wrath.** And He makes their land a **desolation** that people look at with **contempt. Zephaniah 2:15**

Particularly relevant in today's COVID world, God reminds the people that it is He that sends even pandemics so that people will humble themselves and turn from their wicked ways.

When I shut up the heavens so that there is no rain, or command locusts to devour the land *or send a pandemic among my people*, 14 if my people, who are called by my name, will humble themselves and pray and seek my face and turn from their wicked ways, then I will hear from heaven, and I will forgive their sin and will heal their land. 2 Chronicles 7:13-14

We have spent the last year proud of ourselves in our social distancing, our masks, our zoom expertise, and our vaccines, but has our nation or, for that matter, have our churches **humbled themselves** and turned from their **wicked ways**?
We have seen God judge the nations of Philistia, Moab, Cush, and Assyria. Is our nation any different?

Do we really believe that God won't similarly judge us for our idolatry?

Secularism is an empty charade that has intimidated Christians into believing that their religion must stay quiet and safely hidden inside the church. As Gandalf said, *Keep it secret, keep it safe.* We have been taught and are acting as if we believe that the Public Square must remain neutral. But that is a lie. Morality is never neutral. Someone's morality will always prevail; it will either be the bloodlust of the modern secular priests of Baal or the ethic of love for God and neighbor.

If I sit next to a madman as he drives a car into a group of innocent bystanders, I can't, as a Christian, simply wait for the catastrophe, then comfort the wounded... I must try to wrestle the steering wheel out of the hands of the driver. Dietrich Bonhoeffer

How is it that a nation of hundreds of millions of professing Christians have allowed themselves to be intimidated into silence in the face of the great evils of our time? Do we not care for our fellow citizens?

Wisdom cries aloud in the streets,
In the markets she raises her voice'
At the head of the noisy street she cries out;
At the Court she speaks:
How long will you insist on being simpleminded?
How long will you relish mocking?
How long will you hate knowledge?
You ignored my advice.
You rejected correction.
So I will laugh when you are in trouble.
I will mock when disaster overtakes you.
When calamity overtakes you
When disaster engulfs you and
anguish and distress overwhelm you.
you will cry for help and I will not answer.
They anxiously search for Me but will not find Me.

For they hated knowledge
and chose not to fear God.
They rejected My advice
And rejected correction…
Fools are destroyed by their complacency. Proverbs 1:20-33

Will we turn from our sin and confess our complacency? We are to speak out the truth in public. Will God forgive our sin and heal the church or will God remove our lamp stand? **Revelation 2:5**

Just in our lifetime, how many nations that officially rejected the one true God now have growing or majority Christian populations? The Soviet Union, and her Eastern Block Countries were formerly atheistic but no longer. South Korea is a majority Christian nation. China, although officially atheistic, is trying unsuccessfully to repress their growing 300 million Christian population. Even in Muslim nations, where the penalty for leaving Islam is death, many are rejecting Allah and coming to Christ.

As God Promised: **In the last days the mountain of the Lord's house will be established as the highest of the mountains... and peoples will stream to it. Many nations will come and say, "Come, let us go up to the mountain of the Lord, to the house of the God of Jacob. He will teach us his ways, so that we may walk in his paths." The law will go out from Zion, the word of the Lord from Jerusalem. Micah 4:1-2**

All around the world people from every tribe and nation are streaming into Christ's Kingdom, the church, the New Jerusalem. **Revelation 21** They are learning God's **ways**. They are following **His paths**. They are discipling the **nations… teaching them to obey everything [Christ] commanded. Matthew 28:19-20**

Do you understand that Christ expects the nations to **obey** Him?

How can they believe if they have not heard? Romans 10:14

12

Oppressing City

After pronouncing God's judgment on the surrounding nations, Zephaniah returns his focus again to Jerusalem.

Zephaniah 3:1 Woe to her who is rebellious and polluted,
The oppressing city!
2 She heeded not the voice,
She accepted no correction.
She did not trust in the Lord,
She did not draw near to her God.
3 Her princes within her are roaring lions,
Her judges are wolves at evening;
They leave nothing for the morning.
4 Her prophets are reckless, men of deception;
Her priests have profaned the holy place.
They have done violence to the law.
5 The Lord is righteous within her;
He will do no injustice.
Every morning He brings His justice to light;
He does not fail.
But the unjust knows no shame.
6 "I have cut off nations;
Their corner towers are in ruins.
I have made their streets desolate,
With no one passing by;
Their cities are laid waste,
No one dwells there.
7 "I said, 'Surely you will fear Me,
Accept correction.'
So her dwelling will not be cut off
Because of the punishment I have inflicted on her.
But they were eager to corrupt all their deeds.
8 "Therefore wait for Me," declares the Lord,
"For the Day when I rise up to testify.
Indeed, My decision is to gather nations,

To assemble kingdoms,
To pour out on them My indignation,
All My burning anger;
For all the earth will be devoured
By the fire of My zeal.

Why is Jerusalem Judged?

Zephaniah 3:1 Woe to her who is rebellious and unclean,
The oppressing city!
2 She heeded not the voice,
She accepted no correction.
She did not trust in the Lord,
She did not draw near to her God.

In the Old Covenant the priests acted as the representatives of God. Because they represented God they had to follow stringent moral, genealogical, and hygienic requirements. **Leviticus 21** Uncleanness prevented the priest from maintaining his distinctive relationship with God and disqualified the priest from interceding for the people and performing his sacred duties.

Here Zephaniah announces that not only are the priests unclean, but, in fact, the whole population of Jerusalem is unclean. They were to be a kingdom of priests, **Exodus 19:6,** but they were morally polluted. Zephaniah lists four ways that Jerusalem has failed to honor God.

1. She heeded not the voice.

The Chosen, Covenant people of God, were unique among all the nations of the earth because they alone had heard the voice of God.

Ask now about the former days, long before your time, from the day God created human beings on the earth; ask from one end of the heavens to the other. Has anything so great as this ever happened, or has anything like it ever been heard of? 33 Has any

other people heard the voice of God speaking out of fire, as you have, and lived? 34 Has any god ever tried to take for himself one nation out of another nation, by testings, by signs and wonders, by war, by a mighty hand and an outstretched arm, or by great and awesome deeds, like all the things the Lord your God did for you in Egypt before your very eyes?

35 You were shown these things so that you might know that the Lord is God; besides him there is no other. 36 From heaven he made you hear his voice to discipline you.
Deuteronomy 4:32-36

No other nation, Philistia, Moab, Cush, Assyria, no other city, Gaza, Ashkelon, Ashdod, Enron, had been privileged to hear the Word of God. Israel, represented by Jerusalem, alone had heard the voice of God. And yet, even after hearing God's word, experiencing His great salvation and special blessings, and even after entering into a Covenant with God, Judah **heeded not** God's **voice.** As a result she was in danger of judgment: The Day of the Lord.

But it shall come to pass, if thou wilt not hearken unto the voice of the Lord thy God, to observe to do all his commandments and his statutes which I command thee this day; that all these curses shall come upon thee, and overtake thee. Deuteronomy 28:15

The Holy Spirit gives this exact same warning to Christians today:

Therefore, holy brothers and sisters, who share in the heavenly calling, fix your thoughts on Jesus, whom we acknowledge as our apostle and high priest... We are his house, if indeed we hold firmly to our confidence and the hope in which we glory.
As the Holy Spirit says:
"Today, if you hear his voice,
do not harden your hearts
as you did in the rebellion,
during the time of testing in the wilderness,
where your ancestors tested and tried me. Hebrews 3:1-8

Christians are told to listen to God's voice and warned to not follow the example of their ancestors in the faith who rebelled against God and suffered the consequences.

2. She accepted no correction.

Throughout her history God had lovingly corrected and disciplined His wayward nation.

Do not despise the Lord's *discipline* and do not resent his rebuke, because the Lord disciplines those he loves, as a father the son he delights in. Proverbs 3:11-1

As every parent knows, when our children are disobedient or doing things that put their character development or even their lives in danger, we discipline them. This discipline in not a sign of hate or rejection, as children sometimes imagine. Rather discipline is an act of love. Now, being sinful and imperfect parents, we admittedly, sometimes mishandle discipline. Even our best intentions can fail. But not so with our God. God disciplines those whom He loves.

And you have forgotten that word of encouragement that addresses you as sons: "My son, *do not make light of* the Lord's discipline, and do not lose heart when he rebukes you, because the Lord disciplines those he loves, and he punishes everyone he accepts as a son." Endure hardship as discipline; *God is treating you as sons.* For what son is not disciplined by his father? If you are not disciplined (and everyone undergoes discipline), then you are illegitimate children and not true sons. Hebrews 12:5-8

We should not become hardened like the residents of Jerusalem. Because we are sons and daughters of God we are to accept His correction, knowing that He loves us and is guiding us into the fullness of life.

3. She did not trust in the Lord.

The people of Jerusalem had come to believe that trusting in God was not enough. They thought that needed to worship and honor other gods, gods that could somehow provide for them in ways that the Lord could or would not. Not trusting God is nothing less than a rebellious act of treason.

Trust in the Lord with all your heart,
And lean not on your own understanding;
In all your ways acknowledge Him,
And He shall direct your paths. Proverbs 3:5-6

When we are tempted to lean on our own understanding, thinking that we know better than the One who loves us, the One who knows the end from the beginning, **Isaiah 56:10,** we should each remember that:

My God will supply all your needs according to His glorious riches in Christ Jesus. Philippians 4:19

What gods are you trusting in?

The most popular god today is the god of self. You have most likely heard people claim to be following 'their truth' as opposed to following God's truth. Because it fails to correspond to reality, following 'their truth' is nothing more than delusional thinking that frequently leads to unfulfilling lives of pain and futile searching.

4. She did not draw near to her God.

The people of Judah were drawing near to, fleeing to, Baal and Molech. They were offering their time and treasure to these false gods. They were fornicating with the male and female temple prostitutes, sacrificing their children, and donating the fruits of their labor to these gods in exchange for peace, prosperity, and social standing.

We live in a restless and anxious society. We live in a society longing for meaning, purpose, and peace. Do people today spend their time and treasure in seeking after things that will not satisfy the deep longing in their lives? Does ignoring or rewriting God's revelation bring lasting peace? Will following your own truth lead to the real truth that can set you free? Does pornography, adultery, fornication, or sodomy offer lasting satisfaction? Does sacrificing children bring joy or a lasting legacy? Does social standing, spending time and treasure on experiences, pleasures, and possessions truly bring comfort and security either in this life or at the time of death?

Listen to God's offer.

"Come, all you who are thirsty, come to the waters;
and you who have no money, come, buy and eat!
Come, buy wine and milk without money and without cost.
Why spend money on what is not bread, and your labor on what does not satisfy?
Listen, listen to me, and eat what is good, and you will delight in the richest of fare.
Give ear and come to me; listen, that you may live.
I will make an everlasting Covenant with you, my faithful love promised to David.
Isaiah 55:1-3

To all who are thirsting for forgiveness from the sins that ensnare them and the shame that stalks them, thirsting for true meaning, satisfaction, security, love, and joy in life, God asks,

Why spend your labor on what does not satisfy?

What is the alternative?

The alternative is that Christ invites everyone:

Come unto Me all you who are weary and burdened, and I will give you rest. Matthew 11:28

God offers to freely give life to those who draw near to Him: **Come... you who have no money... come to Me, listen, that you may live.**

God is personally inviting you into **an everlasting Covenant** relationship. Like Jerusalem of old, the wages that they have earned for their sin and rebellion against God is wrath, alienation, and death. That is what they and all who sin have earned. But while **the wages of sin is death, the gift of God is eternal life. Romans 6:23**

God is imploring his rebellious children, to **draw near.**

Draw near to God and He will draw near to you. Cleanse *your* hands, *you* sinners; and purify *your* hearts, *you* double-minded. James 4:8

Cleanse your hands; to the residents of Jerusalem as well as to everyone today, that means consider, recount, and confess your sins to God. Come acknowledging that you have followed after other false gods of your making. Gods that you thought could bring you lasting satisfaction. God's that will always fail because they are by nature hollow counterfeit lies. "Your truth" is nothing more than a comforting delusion compared to the God of Truth. Repent and draw near to God for life.

We are half-hearted creatures, fooling around with drink and sex and ambition when infinite joy is offered us, like an ignorant child who wants to go on making mud pies in a slum because he cannot imagine what is meant by the offer of a holiday at the sea. We are far too easily pleased. C.S. Lewis

13

Leadership Judged

After fulfilling his Covenantal duties as God's prosecuting attorney by bringing an indictment against the people of Jerusalem, Zephaniah turns his attention to the leadership. He brings charges against the leadership: the Princes, judges, prophets and priests who were responsible for the decadence in the society.

God is nothing if not realistic. He knows the sinful nature of man. He knows that if that nature is not kept in check evil will run rampant in a land. As such, within the Covenant, God had established a series of checks and balances to restrain and limit the power of the rulers and, thereby, insure justice in the governing of His people.

The King and his Court were to rule by following God's law. They were to read the law daily so that they could rule justly.

The Judges were to judge impartially on the basis of the law.

So that they could understand and obey, people were to stand before the reading of the law every seven years. **Deuteronomy 31:11**

The Priests were to continually speak for God, teaching everyone, including the King and the Judges, God's law.

And, as we have seen, the Prophets were the prosecuting attorneys, bringing God's indictments against those who violated God's law.

Zephaniah3:3 Her Princes within her are roaring lions,
Her Judges are wolves at evening;
They leave nothing for the morning.
4 Her prophets are reckless, men of deception;
Her priests have profaned the holy place.
They have done violence to the law.

Zephaniah first addresses the civil authorities, Princes and Judges.

1. Her Princes within her are roaring lions.

God has established governments to restrain evil. **Romans 13:1-7** However, rather than restraining evil by holding the wicked Kings accountable and shepherding the people, the Princes of Judah were like roaring lions devouring the people.

Your rulers are rebels, and companions of thieves;
Everyone loves a bribe, and chases after rewards.
They do not defend the orphan, nor does the widow's plea come before them. Isaiah 1:23

Her princes within her are like wolves tearing the prey, by shedding blood and destroying lives in order to get dishonest gain. Ezekiel 22:27

When a nation's rulers are thieves and murders only looking out for their own self interest the people of the nation suffer.

When the wicked rule, the people groan. Proverbs 29:2

That is why God taught that it was important for the Princes, that is those who are lesser magistrates; those beneath the King in rank, to hold the King accountable. When, in the course of human events, the King inevitably neglects or misuses the law, as most powerful leaders eventually do, God expects the lesser magistrates to hold the King accountable. God expects those in the King's Court to correct the King's course.

This Biblical idea of checks and balances on those in power has been incorporated into the laws of many nations around the world, particularly since the signing of the Magna Carta in 1215 and accelerating in the 1500's at the time of the Reformation. Perhaps the following example of lesser magistrates and citizens holding a King accountable will sound familiar:

When in the course of human events is becomes necessary for one people to dissolve the political bands which have connected them with another, and to assume among the powers of the earth, the separate and equal station to which the Laws of Nature and Nature's God entitle them, a decent respect to the opinions of mankind requires that they should declare the causes which impel them to the separation.

2. Her Judges are wolves at evening; They leave nothing for the morning.

One of the checks that God had put into place to restrain the potential misuse of power by the ruling class is an independent judiciary. However, in Judah the Judges had become corrupt in the same way that the King and Princes had become corrupt. While the Princes were likened to roaring lions devouring the property and lives of the people, the Judges are compared to ravenous wolves prowling in the darkness. Their insatiable appetites for dishonest gain consumed even the innocent, who came before them seeking justice. The judges were so greedy that they left nothing, devouring everything.

God will not tolerate unjust Judges.

Woe to unjust judges and to those who issue unfair laws, says the Lord, 2 so that there is no justice for the poor, the widows, and orphans. Yes, it is true that they even rob the widows and fatherless children. Isaiah 10:1-2

It is a well known maxim of our modern welfare state that, *"The poor are a gold mine."*

Why?

Because it is very easy to manipulate emotions and guilt to raise money to help the poor, corrupt judges and politicians have learned that it is always to their advantage to keep a population in poverty. These corrupt politicians and their confederates have discovered that it is even easier to appropriate that guilt money for their own purposes. **There is nothing new under the sun. Ecclesiastes 1:9**

In fact, Christ said that, as a general rule, we will be judged by the same standard that we use to judge others.

For in the same way you judge others, you will be judged, and with the measure you use, it will be measured to you. Matthew 7:2

Because the Princes were like roaring lions and the Judges were like ravening wolves, God was about to come in judgment against the wicked leaders. They had an appointment with The Day of the Lord.

In a sinister twist of the metaphor it is actually God who is the roaring lion. The prophet Jeremiah warned:

God has left His hiding place like the lion;
For their land has become a horror
Because of the fierceness of their oppressing sword
And because of His fierce anger. Jeremiah 25:38

Those civil leaders who oppress the people should fear God's anger.

Next, Zephaniah addresses the unfaithful religious leaders beginning first with the prophets.

3. Her prophets are reckless, men of deception.

Prophets were only and ever authorized to speak the words of God. They were the mouthpiece of God to keep the King, Princes, Judges, and Priests from corruption. They were the check that God had put in place to speak justice and to warn of God's sure and coming judgment against injustice, misconduct, and dishonesty. However, the prophets were on the take. As long as they sided with the corrupt Princes and Judges and didn't make waves they were rewarded. They were willing compromise in order to be accepted by the powerful and, no doubt, profit financially from the corruption. Hanging with the cool kids had its advantages. But God saw through their deception:

"From the least to the greatest, all are greedy for gain;
prophets and priests alike, all practice deceit.
They dress the wound of my people as though it were not serious.
'Peace, peace, 'they say, when there is no peace. Jeremiah 6:13-14

To keep the good times rolling they were unwilling to condemn the King, Princes or the Judges as God demanded. They were **men of deception... saying peace, peace,** everything is okay here. Everything is just as God wants things to be, as though the situation was **not serious.**

But the situation was serious. Not only was The Day of the Lord pending, but look at what God had promised for prophets who spoke lies to the nation in God's name.

A prophet who presumes to speak in my name anything I have not commanded, or a prophet who speaks in the name of other gods, is to be put to death. Deuteronomy 18:20

Not only were the prophets making up stuff about God to maintain the status quo, they were speaking false things about Baal and Molech, as if these blind and deaf idols were somehow legitimate and on par with the Lord.

Of course refusing to speak boldly while maintaining the status quo is something the church is very adept at today:

In these times, let us remember the stages that our evangelical leaders have brought us through:
1. There will not be any need to fight.
2. There may come a time when it is necessary to fight.
3. It is too early to fight.
4. It is too late to fight. This is the post-Christian era. Douglas Wilson

There is never a good time to compromise with the false teachings of the culture. The church carries the sword of the Lord, the Word of God. **Revelation 19:14** God promises that the faithful proclamation of that Word, even in the most difficult circumstances, yields the fruit of repentance. **Matthew 3:8** The odds are ever in the favor of the church because our God is a **strong tower. Proverbs 18:10**

Finally, Zephaniah addresses God's earthly representatives, the priests.

4. Her priests have profaned the holy place.
They have done violence to the law.

The priests were given very specific instructions by God as to how to lead the people in worship. All of the elements in the worship were designed to point to the fulfillment of the Promise that God had given Adam and Eve. The Promise, that One, born of woman, would undo the damage and death that they had brought onto the human race. The One who would redeem mankind through His blood sacrifice. Everything in the temple worship pointed to the Promised Son, Jesus Christ. While this is not the place for an exhaustive study, see for example:

The Laver of water for cleansing represented Christ, the living water. **John 7:38**
The lamp stand represented Christ, the light of the world. **John 8:12**
The show bread represented Christ, the bread of life. **John 6:35**
The sacrificial lamb represented Christ, the Lamb of God. **John 1:29**
The Psalms were the songs telling of the salvation of Christ.

I have installed my king on Zion, my holy mountain.
I will proclaim the Lord's decree...You are my Son;
Ask me, and I will make the nations your inheritance,
the ends of the earth your possession. Psalm 2

But instead of pointing the nation to their Savior and God, the priests profaned the temple introducing, among other things, sacred prostitution and offering to the gods, infants as whole burnt sacrifices.

Zephaniah 3:4 The Lord is righteous within her;
5 He will do no injustice.
Every morning He brings His justice to light;
He does not fail.
But the unjust knows no shame.

Both the civil authorities and the religious authorities knew no shame. They had convinced the people that following other gods could actually bring them prosperity and happiness.

Those who can make you believe absurdities can make you commit atrocities. Voltaire

Just a few examples of shameless absurdities we are taught today:
There is no Creator.
There is no Revelation.
The Bible is only a record of man's search for meaning.
Social justice is Biblical justice.
There are many races and they are not equal.
The government's theft of private property and income will bring about prosperity.
God's creation of binary genders is only a social construct.
Children may choose their own gender.
Marriage is not exclusively between one man and one woman.
God's design of the family is a social construct.
Abortion saves lives.
Knowledge, reason, loyalty, reliability, science, math, evidence, productivity, virtue, freedom, Christianity, to name just a few, are inventions of oppressors to keep the oppressed in check.

But God was not about to allow the utter wickedness of His Prophets and Priests to defile His Chosen nation. They may violate His law, the law designed to bless them and give them life, but God promises to remain **righteous** in Judah.

The Lord is faithful. He will establish you and guard you against the evil one. 2 Thessalonians 3:3

When the system of checks and balances has been broken down by corrupt rulers and judges, and even when the people governed refuse to rise up against the corruption, God promises to cut through the darkness and bring His **justice to light.** God declares:

I am the Lord, the God of all flesh. Is anything too difficult for me? Jeremiah 32:37

Even in our times when both the civil leaders and the religious teachers seem out of control, and even if the people being governed refuse to rise up and confront their wicked leaders, God is always in control. He is never taken by surprise. He is always directing even the smallest detail of his plan.

Not one sparrow falls to the ground apart from the will of God. Matthew 10:29

Though the nations and the unfaithful church will flee in fear from The Day of the Lord, God will not fail to judge, discipline, and ultimately save His people.

14

Consider God's Judgments

In order to help them see the severity of their sin and the utter devastation that the coming Day of the Lord will bring, Zephaniah urges the unfaithful civil and religious leaders of Judah to consider how God dealt with their neighbors, the surrounding nations.

Zephaniah 3:6 "I have cut off nations;
Their corner towers are in ruins.
I have made their streets desolate,
With no one passing by;
Their cities are laid waste,
No one dwells there.
7 "I said, 'Surely you will fear Me,
Accept correction.'
So her dwelling will not be cut off
Because of the punishment I have inflicted on her.
But they were eager to corrupt all their deeds.
8 "Therefore wait for Me," declares the Lord,
"For the Day when I rise up to testify.
Indeed, My decision is to gather nations,
To assemble kingdoms,
To pour out on them My indignation,
All My burning anger;
For all the earth will be devoured
By the fire of My zeal.

God destroyed the defenses of the unfaithful nations, tearing down their **towers.** God **laid waste** to their once bustling cities. Their commerce, their banks, their businesses, were all destroyed, leaving **their streets desolate.** Their wealth, worship, families, and joy had become a dystopian nightmare.

You would think that any sane nation seeing how God judged the other surrounding nations with utter destruction would have ample incentive to stop and take stock of their situation. But God seems amazed by the hardness of their hearts: **Surely,** God reasoned with them, **you will fear me and accept correction,** so that you will not experience a similar fate; so that you will **not be cut off.** But, despite seeing God's judgment on the other nations Judah was still **eager to corrupt all their deeds.**

Zephaniah 3:8 "Therefore wait for Me," declares the Lord,
"For the Day when I rise up to testify.
Indeed, My decision is to gather nations,
To assemble kingdoms,
To pour out on them My indignation,
All My burning anger;
For all the earth will be devoured
By the fire of My zeal.

As we have read, Zephaniah began his prophesy by declaring the coming Day of the Lord: A day of cosmic judgment against both the nations and against His unfaithful people, Judah. Josiah had considered God's judgment. He had taken the warnings to heart and instituted reforms. The temple was refurbished and in the process God's Word was rediscovered. Josiah read God's Word aloud to the whole nation. He urged the people to follow God. Josiah destroyed the false idols and the false worship and banished the idolatrous and false priests. And because of Josiah's faithfulness God withheld judgment, however, the repentance of the people did not run deep. It was not genuine. After Josiah's death, the nation of Judah, led by Josiah's unfaithful sons, resumed their idolatrous ways. The worship of Baal was re-instituted.

As a result, the promised destruction of Judah, prophesied in the opening poem of Zephaniah, fell upon the land. The Day of the Lord's judgment arrived in 586 B.C. with the armies of Babylon as God's instrument of punishment. The people who escaped the sword were carried off into captivity as slaves. The curses, described in Deuteronomy, for disobedience to the Covenant, fell upon the people, just as God had warned.

15

God Purifies His People

God had just announced His final decree. He had assembled the nations so that He could pour out His wrath and indignation on them. They were to be devoured. God said that He would:

Pour out on them My indignation,
All My burning anger;
For all the earth will be devoured.
By the fire of My zeal. Zephaniah 3:8

At God's final decree all hope is lost. Or was it?

Just when you might think that all hope is lost, just when you think that the end has come for both the pagan nations and the unfaithful people of God, Zephaniah says something remarkable. Zephaniah talks about God converting the wayward sinful nations and purifying His people.

Zephaniah 3:9 "For then I will convert the nations."

What is going on and where did this come from?

To understand this we must refer back again to the Covenant.

After our first parents, Adam and Eve gave into temptation and followed the wicked lies of Lucifer and sinned against God, rather than giving up on His image bearers, destroying them completely or maybe even starting over, God met with them. God's love for us was so great that He made a Promise to Adam and Eve. God Promised that one day a future Son of Eve would come and both destroy Lucifer and rescue Adam's rebellious race. To insure that this Salvation would happen, to insure that God's Promise was true, throughout history, God entered into Covenants with His people: Adam, Noah, Abraham, Moses, David, and Jeremiah. The Bible calls these the **Covenants of the Promise. Ephesians 2:12**

As we saw, the amazing thing about these Covenants was that, despite the fact that Adam's sinful race would always fail to uphold their end of the Covenant, God swore on Himself, that He would always be faithful to His Promise. **Though we are faithless, He remains faithful, for He cannot deny Himself. 2 Timothy 2:13** God would never give up on His children.

God gave His people a graphic picture of His faithfulness in the Covenant ceremony with Abraham. God instructed Abraham to bring a heifer, a goat, a ram, a dove, and a pigeon to the Covenant ceremony. He was to cut the animals in half and lay the halfs opposite each other on the left and on the right with a path in between. Then God walked between the animals. **Genesis 15:9-21**

This ceremony may be strange to us but for Abraham it was standard operating procedure. It was know as cutting a Covenant. When two rulers entered into a treaty or contract, called a Covenant, they would cut a sacrificial animal into two pieces and then the two rulers would walk between the two split animal pieces. This visually symbolized the fact that both parties were agreeing to the terms of the Covenant and, further, both were saying that should they violate the Covenant oath they would face the same fate as the animal: death.

Today we enter into Covenants such as a mortgage and both parties, the borrower and the lender, acknowledge that they have both rights and responsibilities and will face a penalty for breach of contract.

However, there is one major difference between the normal Covenant ceremony of ancient times and the ceremony in **Genesis 15.** Here both parties did not pass between the sacrificial animal. God alone passed between the animals. By so doing God is swearing on Himself that He swill keep His Promise to Abraham and to all of Abraham's descendants. **When God made His Promise to Abraham He swore the oath on Himself because He had no one greater to swear by. Hebrews 6:13**

God had given a glimpse of what He had planned through these Covenants to the prophet Jeremiah:

The days are coming, declares the Lord, when I will make a New Covenant with the house of Israel and the house of Judah, 32 not like the Covenant that I made with their fathers on the day when I took them by the hand to bring them out of the land of Egypt, my Covenant that they broke, though I was their husband, declares the Lord. Jeremiah 31:31-32

Adam's race has from the beginning been sinful and rebellious, always breaking the Covenant. Though we are God's special creation, made in God's image, and though we aspire to greatness, the history of mankind, even the history of God's chosen people, is a history of arrogance, idolatry, betrayal, greed, war, and **everything that exalts itself against the knowledge of God. 2 Corinthians 10:5**

Notice that God calls Himself the **husband** of His people. That is why He likens our sin to adultery. **You adulterous people! Do you not know that friendship with the world is enmity with God? James 4:4** Like an adulterous spouse, we violate our Covenant marriage oath, when we are unfaithful to God.

But through all of our filth God not only remained faithful, He Promised a New Covenant.

What makes the New Covenant different?

Jeremiah elaborated:

For this is the covenant that I will make with the house of Israel after those days, declares the Lord: I will put my law within them, and I will write it on their hearts. And I will be their God, and they shall be my people. 34 And no longer shall each one teach his neighbor and each his brother, saying, 'Know the Lord, 'for they shall all know me, from the least of them to the greatest, declares the Lord. For I will forgive their iniquity, and I will remember their sin no more. Jeremiah 31:33-34

What does this mean, the law written on hearts?

Although this has been largely forgotten, according to the Bible the law has three functions.

The first function of the law is to show us our inability to keep the law. We all, in one way or another, have a distorted self conception. Because we are adept at self deception we think we are pretty good people. The law of God destroys the myth that we can be good enough to come to God on the basis of our obedience. The law points out our sins, the sins we rationalize away or overlook. Paul noted that it is impossible for us to be righteous. We cannot keep the law of God. Honestly looking at the law exposes our inability to be righteous. **Philippians 3:9**

As St. Augustine observed:

The law bids us, as we try to fulfill its requirements, and we become wreaked in our weakness under it, to know how to ask the help of grace.

Although this is almost universally ignored in the church today, historically, the law and gospel were preached together in the weekly church services. Hearing the requirements of the law strips us of the false idea that we can be good enough to earn our way to God. Having been stripped of our false assurance we understand that our only hope is to be found in the Gospel; Christ's offer of free grace. **The law is our tutor driving us to Christ. Galatians 3:24**

This is clearly seen in **Nehemiah 8.** All of Israel was gathered for worship at the Water Gate. The Book of the Law was then placed on a lectern and read aloud to the nation. In hearing God's Word, **The people wept** in despair. The hammer of the Law was crushing them.

As the Law exposed their sins they grieved, fearing the sure punishment of God. After hearing the Law, as they wept, the priests taught the people how to prepare for the Day of Atonement, the day when a spotless lamb would be sacrificed for their sins, taking the punishment they deserved. Because of Christ, the Lamb of God, represented by the Old Covenant sacrificial lamb, the righteousness of

Christ was imputed to the people, the priests announced, **Do not mourn or weep or grieve, for the joy of the Lord is you strength.**

I do not know when I am more perfectly happy than when I am weeping for sin at the foot of the cross... The fear of God is the death of every other fear; like a mighty lion it chases all other fears before it. C.H. Spurgeon

The second function of the law is to restrain evil in the world. As we saw above, even the unbelieving nations were to be obedient to the law. You would not want to live in a society where murderers, thieves, and other lawless people were not apprehended and brought to justice. The civil code and the sure threat of punishment inhibits lawlessness, making civilization possible. **Romans 13:1-7** This is why God will not be patient with unbelieving nations indefinitely. He judges all nations for their unrighteousness.

The third function of the law shows us what the love of God looks like. Realizing that we have been saved by grace alone because of the sacrificial death of Christ in our place, and understanding that we have been adopted as children into God's family, we look in gratitude toward our Creator and Savior. And, in so doing, we come to understand that the law, based on the perfect character of God, is what the love of God looks like.

The Christian is freed from the law as a means of salvation. We no longer believe in 'works righteousness.' We cannot earn our way into God's family. But having been made a child of God by grace. Because we are created in God's image, we come to realize that living out the law fulfills our deepest longings. It is who we were made to be. It is how we were wired. **Galatians 6:2, 1 Corinthians 9:21**

The Gospel is not a new law.
It is not a code of morals or ethics.
It is not a creed to be accepted.
It is not a system of religion to be adhered to.
It is not good advice to be followed.
It is the Divinely given message concerning the Son of God, Jesus Christ our Lord. H.A.Ironside

To put this another way, as to the first function of the law, every single Christian became a Christian in the same way; justified, freed from the death penalty that their sin deserved. Freed through the perfect obedience of Christ. We all stood before God condemned, unable to offer anything to redeem ourselves. We were shown that: **Our best works are like filthy rags. Isaiah 64:6** Our salvation is an undeserved gift. We have no grounds for boasting. **Ephesians 2:9** We were all in the same boat and it was sinking before God imputed the righteousness of Christ to our account. This is called Justification.

However, the third function of the law is a different story. While Justification is exactly the same for every Christian, Sanctification by the Holy Spirit, the process of being freed from the power of sin, being transformed into Christ's image, taking on the traits of the family, God's family, that we have been adopted into, varies from Christian to Christian. Sanctification is a halting and struggling process as we all wrestle to varying degrees and with varying success with our old sinful nature and old habits, as we unlearn and discard destructive thoughts, attitudes, and behaviors and learn to imitate the ways of Christ. **Ephesians 5:1**

Now what is salvation? Some people think that it means being saved from going down to hell. That is the result of salvation; but salvation means being saved from the power of sin, and being saved from the tendency to sin, as well as being saved from the punishment of sin. C.H. Spurgeon

In Christ we have been provided the **double cure**. He has saved us from the wrath of God's judgment by Christ's sacrifice for us; the wrath of The Day of the Lord. And now, He works in our lives to remake and restore us in Sanctification, as we cling to our rock and Savior. In the words of the hymn, Rock of Ages, written by Augustus Toplady in 1763:

Rock of Ages, cleft for me,
Let me hide myself in Thee;
Let the water and the blood,
Form Thy riven side which flowed,
***Be of sin the* double cure,**

Save from wrath and make me pure.

The picture of the long awaited Lamb of God first shown to us in the sacrifice in **Genesis 3:21** has been fulfilled in Christ. His once for all time, sacrifice of our behalf, **Revelation 13:8** is the only means of our Justification.

Christ explained to His disciples that after He went to heaven God would send the Holy Spirit to live within His followers: **And I will pray the Father, and He shall give you another Comforter, that He may abide with you for ever. John 14:16**

And according to the Apostle Peter that is exactly what happened. God **poured out His Spirit on all flesh, Acts 2:17;** the means of our Sanctification.

Again, because this is widely misunderstood today, I must add one quick clarification of the law. The Old Covenant law consisted of three parts, ceremonial, civil and moral.

Christ said that He came to **fulfill the law. Matthew 5:17-20**

Ceremonial Laws: As we noted, all of the Temple and sacrifices looked forward to Christ. Because in His ultimate sacrifice, all of the ceremonial laws were fulfilled, the Church no longer practices the Old Covenant ceremonial laws. The book of **Hebrews** explains this in great detail.

Civil Laws: These were the laws that God gave to His nation Israel and dealt with such things as rulers and authorities, boundaries, crime and punishment, marriage and divorce, and all other civil matters. Even though the nations of the world are not Israel, because these laws are from God, much can be learned from them. For example, as we have seen, many nations have adopted God's system of checks and balances to restrain evil.

Moral Law: The clearest example of the moral law is the Ten Commandments and the Case Law derived from them recorded in Exodus. As we saw above, God expects even unbelieving nations to follow His moral law and He will hold accountable those nations and peoples who do not follow His moral law.

Much more could be said to clarify God's law and its application, and, in fact, countless volumes have been written, but we must always remember Christ's concise explanation of the Law:

Love the Lord your God with all your heart and all your soul and all your mind… and love your neighbor as yourself.
Matthew 22:38-39

For by the law we see our misery, and by the Gospel our remedy.
Edmund Calamy

16

God Converts the Nations

Next, amazingly, Zephaniah foresees, not only the salvation of God's people, Judah, but also the salvation of the nations of the world.

Zephaniah 3:9 "For then I will convert the nations
So that they speak with purified lips,
That they may call on the name of the Lord,
To serve Him shoulder to shoulder.
10 "From beyond the rivers of Ethiopia
My worshipers, My dispersed ones,
Will bring My offerings.
11 "In that day you will feel no shame
Because of all your deeds
By which you have rebelled against Me;
For then I will remove from your midst
Your proud, exulting ones,
And you will never again be haughty
On My holy mountain.12 "But I will leave among you
A humble and poor people,
Who will seek shelter in the name of the Lord.
13 "The remnant of Israel will not do evil,
Will speak no lies,
Nor will a deceitful tongue
Be found in their mouths;
For they will feed and lie down
With no one to make them afraid."

In His Covenant with Abraham God made an astonishing Promise:

Through you all the nations of the world will be blessed. Genesis 22:18

What could this mean?

God revealed more details to the Prophet Isaiah:

In that day the Root of Jesse will stand as a banner for the peoples; the nations will rally to Him, and his resting place will be glorious. 11 In that day the Lord will reach out His hand a second time to reclaim the surviving remnant of his people from Assyria, from Lower Egypt, from Upper Egypt, from Cush, from Elam, from Babylonia, from Hamath and from the islands of the Mediterranean.

12 He will raise a banner for the nations and gather the exiles of Israel; He will assemble the scattered people of Judah from the four quarters of the earth. Isaiah 11:10-12

All the nations will rally to **the Root of Jesse,** Jesus Christ. Even the scattered people of Judah will return to God.

Zephaniah 3:9 "For then I will convert the nations
So that they speak with purified lips,
That they may call on the name of the Lord,
To serve Him shoulder to shoulder.
10 "From beyond the rivers of Ethiopia
My worshipers, My dispersed ones,
Will bring My offerings.

The nations will be converted. They will come to God. This is exactly what the resurrected and victorious Christ told His disciples:

Go and make disciples of all nations, baptizing them in the name of the Father and of the Son and of the Holy Spirit, and teaching them to obey everything I have commanded you.
Matthew 28:19-20

Instead of futilely relying on their good works to repair their broken relationship with God, or instead of chasing after gods that cannot satisfy, the people of the nations were **converted.** They came to trust in Christ alone for their salvation: **There is salvation in no one else; for there is no other name under heaven that has been given among men by which we must be saved. Acts 4:12**

But Zephaniah not only mentions their conversion, their Justification. He next points to their Sanctification. Through the outpouring of the Holy Spirit they were **putting on the new self, created for righteousness and holiness in the truth. Ephesians 2:24** Or as Zephaniah poetically describes it, they were now able to speak with **purified lips.**

I will cleanse you from all your impurities and from all your idols. Ezekiel 36:25

But not only was their speech changed but their lives have changed as well as they **serve Him shoulder to shoulder.**

There are many forces in the world today that are trying to divide people and drive people apart on the basis of race, ethnicity, gender, politics, religion, education, economics, and much, much more. The last thing that Satan wants is for the people of the nations to unite under the banner of Christ. Satan strives to keep people divided by hostilities, suspicion, and recrimination. In contrast, look at the beautiful picture Zephaniah paints: people serving the true God **shoulder to shoulder.** Paul asks the nations to:

Remember that at that time you were separate from Christ and excluded from citizenship in Israel. Foreigners to the Covenants of the Promise, without hope and without God in the world. But now in Christ Jesus you who were once far away have been brought near by the blood of Christ... He has made the two groups one having destroyed the dividing wall of hostility... He put to death hostility... We are no longer foreigners and strangers, but instead are fellow citizens within the household. Ephesians 1:12-19

Christ has granted **citizenship** to the people of all nations. Christians, regardless of nation, or race, or ethnicity, are no longer strangers. The **hostility** of all artificial divisions, Jew and Greek, barbarian or Scythian, slave or free, male or female, **Galatians 3:28, Colossians 3:11,** are now melted away in Christ. Christians are in one **household**, one family, **fellow citizens** with Christ. We who were once strangers now love each other in Christ as brothers and sisters. **1 John 3:14-16**

We are devoted to each other. **Romans 12:10** We consider how to encourage each other in kindness, love, and good works. **Hebrews 10:24**

In **Genesis,** because of the sinful nature of man, in order to restrain the damage that sinful man could do, God created the nations and languages, and scattered humanity across the face of the globe. **Genesis 11:1-9** Here, finally, that judgment is reversed. Because of the faithfulness of Christ, God is now able to gather His scattered children from all the nations together into His **household;** the church.

Zephaniah 3:10 "From beyond the rivers of Ethiopia
My worshipers, My dispersed ones, Will bring My offerings.

But there is more. Not only will God unite the peoples of all the scattered nations into His Kingdom, He will remove their shame from them. The shame they experienced for all of their sinful, idolatrous deeds will be removed.

Where once there was shame for **the wicked deeds done in darkness, Ephesians 5:11,** God has granted forgiveness through Christ. Not only are our sins forgiven, **as far as the east is from the west, so far are our sins removed from us, Psalm 103:12,** and not only are we a **new creation, 2 Corinthians 5:17**, no longer captive to our old sins, habits, failures, and attitudes, but God has also removed our shame; the shame we feel for our former sins, failings, deeds, attitudes, shortcomings, and rebellion: the shame that we hide.

Zephaniah 3:11 "In that day you will feel no shame
Because of all your deeds
By which you have rebelled against Me;
For then I will remove from your midst
Your proud, exulting ones,
And you will never again be haughty
On My holy mountain.

Shame is a grace of God that leads to true repentance. When we proudly and shamelessly walk in our sins it is by grace that God wakes us up through rebuke and at times mocking, to help us see the utter wickedness of the sins we, in deceit, embrace. **God laughs at them and taunts them. Psalm 2:4, Proverbs 1**

Our sins have been atoned for. We have been given new hearts. We are freed from shame. We have been enfolded into a loving and accepting community along with others who have also been forgiven, made new, and freed from shameful sins.

I was recently speaking to a young man who stated that he believed in God. To help him clarify his thoughts I asked him if he was sure he would go to heaven after his death. He stated that he hoped that he would. When I asked him what he based that hope on he responded that he tried to be a good person and that he hoped that the good would counterbalance the evil that he had done.

Just as in **Nehemiah 8** where the hammer of the law exposed the sin of the people, I began to remind the young man of the Ten Commandments. Had he ever lied? Had he ever stolen or been dishonest in a transaction? Had he cheated on his wife? Did he honor his parents? His honest answers revealed to him both his shame and his haughty attitude. He had deceived himself about the seriousness of his rebellion against God and, as a result, had convinced himself that he was good enough to deserve a place in heaven. After the law had exposed him, I explained to him **how the Lord laid on Christ the iniquity of us all. Isaiah 53:6.** My friend then came to understand that, **The wages of his sin deserved death.** However he was surprised when he learned **the gift of God is eternal life through Jesus Christ, the Lord. Romans 6:23**

The Gospel… a gift… for free…let that sink in.

Just as Zephaniah had declared to the repentant nations, their rebel deeds and their proud and haughty attitudes toward sin had been removed. The people no longer need to feel shame.

Zephaniah 3:12 "But I will leave among you
A humble and poor people,
Who will seek shelter in the name of the Lord.
13 "The remnant of Israel will not do evil,

Will speak no lies,
Nor will a deceitful tongue
Be found in their mouths;
For they will feed and lie down
With no one to make them afraid."

Having had our sins exposed we are now **a humble and poor people.** We **seek shelter in the name of the Lord** because as we have seen, **there is no other name under heaven given to people by which we must be saved. Acts 4:12**

How can it be said that;

The remnant of Israel will not do evil, Will speak no lies,
Nor will a deceitful tongue, Be found in their mouths?

Remember, the first use of the law exposes our sin, hammers us, and drives us away from our pride and drives us to Christ: Justification.

As Paul would tell the converts from the nations, they no longer needed to feel shame for their past sins: sexual immorality, idolatry, adultery, homosexuality, effeminacy, theft, greed, drunkenness, abusiveness, cheating, swindling, and much more. Paul reminded them, **Such were some of you. But you were washed, you were sanctified, you were justified in the name of the Lord Jesus Christ and by the Spirit of our God. 1 Corinthians 6:9-11**

This is an important phrase: **Such were some of you...**

If you claim to love Christ and yet are living an unholy life: there is only one thing to say about you. You are a bare-faced liar.
Dr. Martyn Lloyd-Jones

The one who says I know Christ, and yet does not keep His commandments, is a liar, and the truth is not in him. 1 John 2:4

Because the believers from the nations are Justified through Christ and Sanctified through the Holy Spirit, they are in the process of being freed from their old destructive sins and habits.

If anyone is in Christ, he is a new creation, the old has passed away. 2 Corinthians 5:17

They are learning of, and living in, the freedom of God's law, written in their hearts, **Jeremiah 31:33,** on **God's holy mountain.** And remember for New Covenant Christians, **God's holy mountain** is none other than the church of Jesus Christ.

You have come to Mount Zion, to the city of the living God, the heavenly Jerusalem. You have come to thousands upon thousands of angels in joyful assembly, to the Church of the firstborn, whose names are written in heaven. Hebrews 12:22-23

God's Promise to Abraham is now being fulfilled. The nations of the earth are being blessed as they stream to the banner of Christ on **God's holy mountain...the Church of the firstborn.**

The Lord, whom you seek, shall suddenly come to His temple, the messenger of the Covenant, whom you delight in: behold He shall come. Malachi 3:1

The Desire of all nations shall come. Haggai 2:7

He will lift up a banner for the nations and gather the exiles. Isaiah 11:12

I have redeemed you; I have called you by name, you are mine. Isaiah 43:1

As Christ Promised:

When I am lifted up from the earth, I will draw all men to Myself. John 12:32

17

God Sings

Zephaniah, who began his prophesy with what is one of most damning judgments in the entire Bible:

Zephaniah 1:2 "I will completely remove all *things*
From the face of the earth," declares the Lord.
3 "I will remove man and beast;
I will remove the birds of the sky
And the fish of the sea,
And the stumbling blocks along with the wicked;
And I will cut off man from the face of the earth," declares the Lord;

ends his prophesy with the most beautiful picture of God's love found in the Bible.

Zephaniah 3:14 Sing for joy, O daughter of Zion!
Shout *in triumph*, O Israel!
Rejoice and be jubilant with all *your* heart,
O daughter of Jerusalem!
15 The Lord has taken away *His* punishments against you,
He has turned back your enemies.
The King of Israel, the Lord, is in your midst;
You will fear disaster no more.
16 In that day it will be said to Jerusalem:
"Do not be afraid, O Zion;
Do not let your hands fall limp.
17 "The Lord your God is in your midst,
A victorious warrior.
He will delight over you with joy,
He will quiet you with His love,
He will rejoice over you with singing.
18 "I will gather those who grieve about the appointed feasts—
They came from you, *O Zion*;
***The* reproach *of exile* is a burden on them.**
19 "Behold, I am going to deal at that time

With all your oppressors,
I will save the lame
And gather the outcast,
And I will turn their shame into praise and renown
In all the earth.
20 "At that time I will bring you in,
Even at the time when I gather you together;
Indeed, I will give you renown and praise
Among all the peoples of the earth,
When I restore your fortunes before your eyes,"
Says the Lord.

The Lord is now in our midst. As God revealed to Jeremiah and as Peter explained on the day of Pentecost, in the New Covenant the Holy Spirit has been poured out on all who repent of their sins and trust in Christ. Again, the Lord now dwells with His people!

Zephaniah 3:14 Sing for joy, O daughter of Zion!
Shout *in triumph*, O Israel!
Rejoice and be jubilant with all *your* heart,
O daughter of Jerusalem!
15 The Lord has taken away *His* punishments against you,
He has turned back your enemies.
The King of Israel, the Lord, is in your midst;
You will fear disaster no more.
16 In that day it will be said to Jerusalem:
"Do not be afraid, O Zion;
Do not let your hands fall limp.

God has taken away the punishments that we deserve and is now living with us, in our midst. We have no reason to fear. God has done that which was impossible for us to do for ourselves. **The wages of sin is death, Romans 6:23,** but Christ paid our debt.

Sing for joy... shout in triumph... rejoice and be jubilant with all your heart.

Have you ever been paralyzed by worst-case scenario thinking? Have you ever been gripped by anxiety?

Have you even gone limp from fear?

Have you ever felt that things were out of control?

As we grow in the knowledge of God, Christ delivers us from fear with joy. Christ, who overcame death on our behalf, is in control.

Although they were afraid and let their anxiety overwhelm them the disciples learned that because Christ was in the boat with them, the storm they feared was irrelevant.

A furious squall came up, and the waves broke over the boat, so that it was nearly swamped. Jesus was in the stern, sleeping on a cushion. The disciples woke him and said to him, "Teacher, don't you care if we drown?" He got up, rebuked the wind and said to the waves, "Quiet! Be still!" Then the wind died down and it was completely calm. He said to his disciples, "Why are you so afraid? Do you still have no faith?" Mark 5:35-41

Similarly, Christ is with us, and asks; **Why are you so afraid?**

Christ promises; **He will quiet you with His love. Zephaniah 3:17**

It is Christ's joy to save us.

**Zephaniah 3:17 "The Lord your God is in your midst,
A victorious warrior.
He will delight over you with joy,
He will quiet you with His love,
He will rejoice over you with singing.**

Christ is **a victorious warrior.** He came, as Promised to Adam and Eve, **to destroy the works of the devil. 1 John 3:8.** He came to defeat our oldest enemy **death. 2 Timothy 1:10, Isaiah 25:8**

Why did Jesus leave heaven and endure the cross?

Jesus... for the joy set before Him, endured the cross, scorning its shame. Hebrews 12:2

What is the joy that Christ kept before Him?

You are the joy.

You are the prize.

You are the reason that Christ **made himself nothing by taking the very nature of a servant, being made in human likeness. And being found in appearance as a man, he humbled himself by becoming obedient to death—even death on a cross! Philippians 2:7-8**

Christ became a man and endured torture and death so that He could redeem you and present you to His Father. God the Father is inheriting a glorious gift from His Son. And that glorious gift, which the Son paid for within His life, is you. **Christ purchased us with His blood, Galatians 3:13,** brought us into His family, placed us in community, and is making us an everlasting delight to God the Father.

He will rejoice over you with singing.

The Son left heaven on a mission to redeem us. Satan, though he tried, could not thwart the Son. Satan tried to have Herod murder the new born child. **Matthew 2:16** Satan tempted Christ to abandon His mission. **Matthew 4:1-11** Satan manipulated the authorities to crucify Christ. **Matthew 27** But Christ triumphed as the victorious warrior; our warrior. He saves us. He quiets us with His love. And because of His faithfulness God now delights in us.

God sings with joy when the Son presents us, those saved by Grace, to the Father.

And God invites us to join in and sing with Him. But there was a time when the people could not join in and sing.
Zephaniah 3:18 "I will gather those who grieve about the appointed feasts—

They came from you, *O Zion*;
***The* reproach *of exile* is a burden on them.**

This is a reference to the Day of the Lord, the day when Judah was taken captive by Babylon in 586 B.C. and exiled. The people mourned the loss of the temple and mourned the loss of their feast days.

By the rivers of Babylon we sat and wept
when we remembered Zion.
There on the poplars we hung our harps,
for there our captors asked us for songs,
our tormentors demanded songs of joy;
they said, "Sing us one of the songs of Zion!"
How can we sing the songs of the Lord
while in a foreign land? Psalm 137:1-4

The Babylonians demanded that their Judaean slaves sing for them. But because of their captivity their joy had turned to mourning.

But Zephaniah announces that there will be a time when God will gather the exiles and they will return to Judah. And after 70 years in captivity that is just what happened. They were allowed to return to Jerusalem. But that was only a foretaste of the final fulfillment of Zephaniah's prophesy.

As we have seen, the greater event to which Zephaniah looked forward to was, not just the return of the Jewish people to their homeland, but the return of the nations of the world to their homeland, the Kingdom of God. The personal relationship that Adam and Eve squandered, the Kingdom of God that they lost, is now being gathered and restored through Christ.

The reproach of exile is now gone, not only for Judah but for the people in the entire world.

Can you see why God is singing?

Can you see why God wants you to join with Him in singing the songs of Zion; the songs of salvation?

Zephaniah 3:19 "Behold, I am going to deal at that time
With all your oppressors,
I will save the lame
And gather the outcast,
And I will turn their shame into praise and renown
In all the earth.

Isaiah had told of a time when the outcasts would be saved; **Isaiah 61.** And when Christ began His work on earth He read the exact same passage to announce His ministry:

The Spirit of the Lord is on me,
because he has anointed me
to proclaim good news to the poor.
He has sent me to proclaim freedom for the captives
and recovery of sight for the blind,
to set the oppressed free,
to proclaim the year of the Lord's favor. Luke 4:18-19

Since the beginning, mankind has been held captive to the lies of Lucifer.

The two great pillars upon which the kingdom of Satan is erected are ignorance and error... It is one of the arch devices and principal methods of Satan to deceive men into sin: thus he prevailed against our first parents, not as a lion, but as a serpent, acting his enmity under the presence of friendship, and tempting them to evil under the appearance of good... ***My people are destroyed for lack of knowledge. Hosea 4:6*** *Westminster Confession of Faith, p4*

But Christ came to **proclaim freedom for the captives... that they will come to their senses and escape from the trap of the devil, who has taken them captive to do his will. 2 Timothy 2:26**

Zephaniah 3:20 "At that time I will bring you in,
Even at the time when I gather you together;

Indeed, I will give you renown and praise
Among all the peoples of the earth,
When I restore your fortunes before your eyes," Says the Lord.

How will we have renown and praise?

Peter explains:

Live such good lives among the pagans that, though they accuse you of doing wrong, they may see your good deeds and glorify God... 1 Peter 2:12

What's does Peter mean?

Quite naturally the unbelievers, the folks that Peter calls the pagans, follow the teaching and logic of the father of lies, the one who accuses Christians of wrongdoing, **Revelation 12:10,** Lucifer.

One of the oldest deceptions in Lucifer's catalogue is convincing people that they are not bad and certainly don't deserve the wrath of God. Be honest. You know yourself. While we don't like to admit it, we all know our lies, our devils, our deeds, and our deceptions; things that we tell ourselves to convince ourselves that compared to that other guy, we are not really bad at all.

Like the father of lies, we are accusers. We look at others and in an attempt to deflect our guilt we accuse others. When unbelievers look at Christians and see the Christians living and sinning just like them they conclude that Christianity is hollow and worthless. Peter issues a warning asking:

If Christians are really no different from pagans in their behavior, how can Christianity be true or worthwhile?

Unbelievers think that Christianity is you doing all the righteous things you hate and avoiding all the wicked things you love in order to go to heaven. No, that's a lost man with religion. A Christian is a person whose heart has been changed; they have new affections.
Paul Washer

Before we were Christians we were chasing after all kinds of experiences and idols, seeking after happiness, fulfillment and peace of mind. But somehow our idols, our friends, our experiences, and our behaviors never could give us the lasting satisfaction that we longed for.

Why?

We were created to do more than just seek fleeting pleasures.

God has set eternity in our hearts. Ecclesiastes 3:11

As St, Augustine explained it:

You have made us for Yourself, O Lord, and our hearts are restless until we find rest in You.

The Apostle Paul puts it like this:

Do not conform to the pattern of this world, but be transformed by the renewing of your mind. Romans 12:2

In other words stop clinging to those idols that could never satisfy: self, greed, possessions, power, sexual immorality, mind altering drugs, seeking the accolades and approval of others; **the pattern of this world.** Instead we are to be made new through the indwelling of the Holy Spirit **renewing our minds.** Our hearts are changed through the process of Sanctification. The Holy Spirit changes our way of thinking and acting.

How will we have **renown and praise among all the peoples of the earth**?

As the people living in the nations come to God the world will notice.

You are the light of the world. A town built on a hill cannot be hidden. 15 Neither do people light a lamp and put it under a bowl. Instead they put it on its stand, and it gives light to everyone in

the house. 16 In the same way, let your light shine before others, that they may see your good deeds and glorify your Father in heaven. Matthew 5:14-16

Unbelievers, seeing the changes in our lives, the changes in our attitudes, the changes in our actions, and our genuine and lasting joy, will take notice. As they notice these things their accusations against will ring hollow. Some of the unbelievers, longing for forgiveness, longing for freedom from their shame, freedom from the fear and uncertainty of death, longing for meaning, purpose, and security in their lives, will listen when they hear of our relationship with the Savior. They will listen when they learn of our assurance of salvation. And some will **see your good deeds and glorify your Father in heaven.**

The whole process is actually counterintuitive. We rationalize that we can attract unbelievers to the Kingdom of God by becoming like them. But as Os Guinnes pointed out, the churches *passion for relevance will become its road to irrelevance.*

In other words:

Scripture does not come alive when we twist it to say what the world desires to hear. Scripture comes alive when our lives are conformed to it. Dustin Benge

As we boldly and valiantly speak and live the truth that God, by grace, has given us, God says:

I restore your fortunes before your eyes.

18

The New Covenant

For Judah, under the Old Covenant, **restoring your fortune before your eyes,** meant being returned from exile and repossessing their land. But, as we have seen, the Old Covenant was just a picture, a foretaste, a shadow, a placeholder, of the true **restoration of fortunes,** Promised in the New Covenant. The shadows of the Old Covenant, such as the sacrificial lamb, are finally and fully fulfilled in Christ, the true Lamb of God. The true Lamb was slain to cover the sins, not only of Judah, but to cover the sins of the world, making it possible for the **nations to come to the light** of Christ's church.

The Church is God's Plan A and there is no Plan B... Christ's first words in the Gospels were straightforward, **repent for the kingdom of heaven is at hand, Matthew 3:2.** *John Stonestreet*

Christ fulfilled all of the conditions of the Covenant of the Promise; the Promise made to our first parents, the Promise that was carefully unfolded throughout the pages of Scripture.

1. Christ identified Himself as Sovereign:
I am the way the truth and the life. John 14:6

2. Christ recounted the mighty deeds that He had done throughout history on behalf of His people.
Because I live you will live also. John 14:19

3. Christ gave laws by which mankind could live productive and joyful lives.
If you love me you will keep my commandments. John 14:15

4. His people took an oath agreeing to both blessings for obedience and curses for disobedience. **All who call on the name of the Lord will be saved. Romans 10:13**

5. God promised to be with and save the future generations of His faithful Covenant children.

Peter replied, "Repent and be baptized, every one of you, in the name of Jesus Christ for the forgiveness of your sins. And you will receive the gift of the Holy Spirit. 39 The promise is for you and your children and for all who are far off—for all whom the Lord our God will call."
Acts 2:38-39

Although many don't realize it, the Church re-enacts this Covenant ceremony in their weekly worship.

The Lord Jesus, on the night he was betrayed, took bread, 24 and when he had given thanks, he broke it and said, "This is my body, which is for you; do this in remembrance of me." 25 In the same way, after supper he took the cup, saying, "This cup is the New Covenant in my blood; do this, whenever you drink it, in remembrance of me." 26 For whenever you eat this bread and drink this cup, you proclaim the Lord's death until he comes.
27 So then, whoever eats the bread or drinks the cup of the Lord in an unworthy manner will be guilty of sinning against the body and blood of the Lord. 28 Everyone ought to examine themselves before they eat of the bread and drink from the cup. 29 For those who eat and drink without discerning the body of Christ eat and drink judgment on themselves. 30 That is why many among you are weak and sick, and a number of you have fallen asleep. 31 But if we were more discerning with regard to ourselves, we would not come under such judgment. 32 Nevertheless, when we are judged in this way by the Lord, we are being disciplined so that we will not be finally condemned with the world.
1 Corinthians 11:23-32

Compare Christ's statement to the points of the Covenant:

1. Sovereign: The Lord Jesus
2. Mighty Deeds: His body was broken for us
3. Law: Do this in remembrance
4. Blessing/Curse: Eat with discernment or face judgment

5. Future: Until He comes

Since the creation God has been working to create a people for Himself, a people who would be identified as His people in the midst of the nations; who would walk in obedience before Him; through whom He would display His glory to the nations; and by whom He would bless all the families of the earth. T.M. Moore

God desires to fill the earth with men and women who will pursue and glorify Him. However, man has always failed to be faithful to this task. We cannot please God. However, as we have seen again and again through the Scripture, God intervenes and establishes His Covenants of the Promise to create a people for Himself.

God remains faithful even though we are unfaithful. Adam sinned, yet God Promised to crush evil and redeem man. Noah's generation rejected God yet God Promised to preserve the earth. Abraham worshiped idols yet God Promised to bless all the nations through him. Israel could not be faithful to the law revealed to Moses yet God established them as a nation of priests. David sinned against God yet God Promised a Kingdom that would endure forever. Zephaniah confronts the people with the consequences of their disobedience, The Day of the Lord's judgment, yet God Promised that the nations will be converted.

The people could never keep the Old Covenant, yet with Christ, God has seen to it, through the New Covenant, that man is no longer in that position. But understand, the New Covenant was not meant to replace the Old Covenant, rather the New Covenant completed the Old Covenant. In the New Covenant we find the final fulfillment of the Promise.

The New Covenant is the same as the Old however the difference is that God has, through Christ, insured that the Covenant will be kept. Through Christ we have the law written on our hearts. We have the Spirit living in our hearts. God is with us to teach us of our sin and to shepherd us to Christ. And finally, because of the death of Christ, God remembers our sins no more. Having given us all this, we are now freed from the slavery of sin and enabled to fulfill God's purpose for His creation; bringing the nations into the Kingdom.

Though these truths are being forgotten by today's shallow churches as they strive for relevance in a secular world, listen to our forefathers in the faith as they describe the Covenant.

Christ by His obedience and death, did fully discharge the debt of all those that are justified, and did make a proper, real and full satisfaction to His Father's Justice in their behalf... God did from all eternity, decree to justify all the elect; Christ did, in the fullness of time, die for their sins, and rise again for their justification... God doth continue to forgive the sins of those that are justified; and although they can never fall from the state of justification, yet may by their sins fall under God's fatherly displeasure, and not have the light of His countenance restored to them, until they humble themselves, confess their sins, beg pardon, and renew their repentance... The justification of believers under the Old Testament was, in all respects, one and the same justification of believers under the New Testament.
Westminster Confession of Faith, Justification XI

They who are effectually called and regenerated, having a new heart and a new spirit created in them, are farther Sanctified really and personally, through the virtue of Christ's death and resurrection, by His Word and Spirit dwelling in them; the dominion of the whole body of sin is destroyed, and the several lusts thereof are more and more weakened and mortified, and they more and more quickened and strengthened in all saving graces, to the practice of true holiness, without which no man shall see the Lord.
Westminster Confession of Faith, Sanctification XIII

Read again the promise made through the Prophet Isaiah:

Arise, shine, for your light has come,
and the glory of the Lord rises upon you.
See, darkness covers the earth
and thick darkness is over the peoples,
but the Lord rises upon you
and his glory appears over you.

Nations will come to your light,
and kings to the brightness of your dawn.
Lift up your eyes and look about you:
All assemble and come to you;
your sons come from afar,
and your daughters are carried on the hip.
Then you will look and be radiant,
your heart will throb and swell with joy;
the wealth on the seas will be brought to you,
to you the riches of the nations will come. Isaiah 60:1-5

Or as Zephaniah so eloquently put it:

Zephaniah 3:20 "At that time I will bring you in,
Even at the time when I gather you together;
Indeed, I will give you renown and praise
Among all the peoples of the earth,
When I restore your fortunes before your eyes,"
Says the Lord.

The Promise made of Adam's Son,
Has had revealed its meaning.
The Light of Christ; salvations' come.
The dark of night is fleeting.
The Covenant of the One,
Into the earth is streaming.
The weak, the lost, the blind, the dumb,
Awaken from their sleeping.
The scattered nations one become.
The enlightened world is seeing,
Hollow pursuits and lies undone.
They never could bring healing.
All of Satan's schemes succumb.
The captives, Christ is freeing;
Once under the deceiver's thumb,
Now to God are pleasing.
Hear as the heavenly chorus drums.
God Rejoices with us singing!